CW01597017

To Borneo and Back

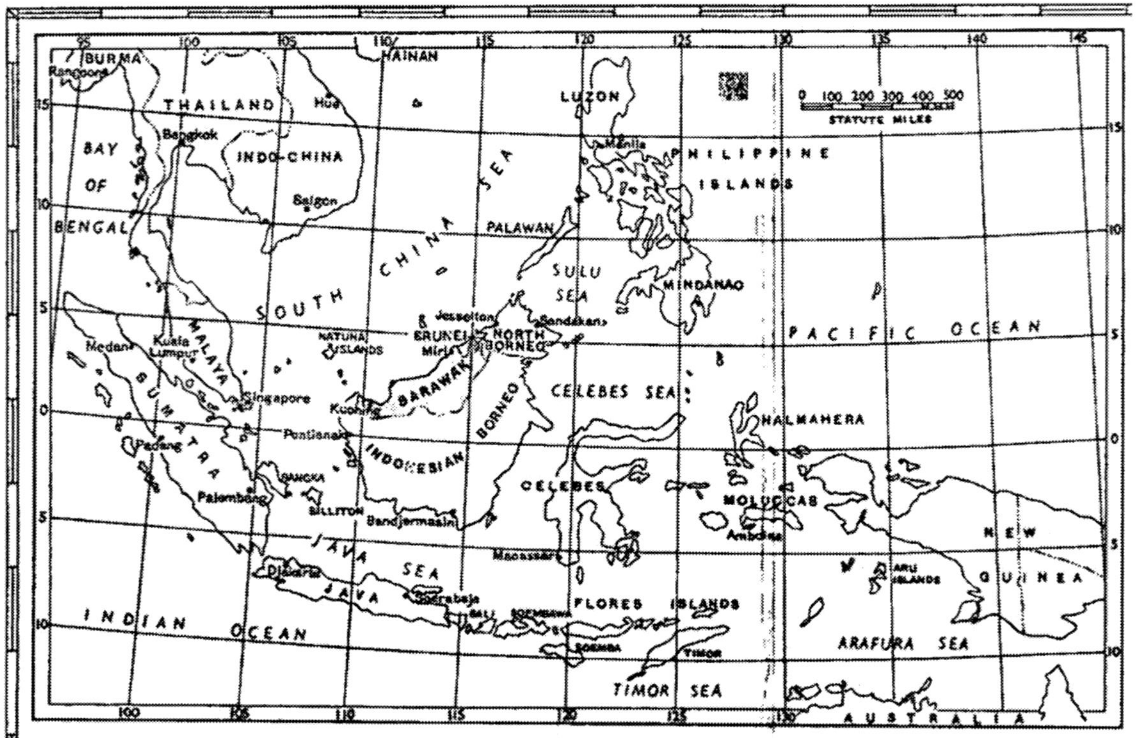

BURMA
Rangoon
THAILAND
Bangkok
INDO-CHINA
Hue
Saigon
HAINAN
BAY OF BENGAL
SOUTH CHINA SEA
MALAYA
Kuala Lumpur
Singapore
SUMATRA
Medan
Padang
Palembang
BANGKA
BILLITON
Pontianak
Kuching
NATUNA ISLANDS
SARAWAK
BRUNEI
Miri
Jesselton
NORTH BORNEO
Sandakan
BORNEO
INDONESIAN
Bandjermasin
JAVA SEA
JAVA
Djakarta
Soerabaja
BALI
SOEMBAWA
SOEMBA
FLORES ISLANDS
TIMOR
TIMOR SEA
INDIAN OCEAN
LUZON
Manila
PHILIPPINE ISLANDS
PALAWAN
SULU SEA
MINDANAO
CELEBES SEA
CELEBES
Macassar
HALMAHERA
MOLUCCAS
Amboina
PACIFIC OCEAN
NEW GUINEA
ARU ISLANDS
ARAFURA SEA
AUSTRALIA
0 100 200 300 400 500
STATUTE MILES

To Borneo and Back

An Encounter with Dietrich Bonhoeffer

James R. Hipkins

iUniverse, Inc.
New York Lincoln Shanghai

To Borneo and Back
An Encounter with Dietrich Bonhoeffer

All Rights Reserved © 2004 by James R. Hipkins

No part of this book may be reproduced or transmitted in any form or by any means, graphic, electronic, or mechanical, including photocopying, recording, taping, or by any information storage retrieval system, without the written permission of the publisher.

iUniverse, Inc.

For information address:
iUniverse, Inc.
2021 Pine Lake Road, Suite 100
Lincoln, NE 68512
www.iuniverse.com

ISBN: 0-595-30845-7

Printed in the United States of America

To Jill Elaine Hipkins Pond and Thomas Corwin Hipkins who accompanied us for much of the journey. They were willing companions for a unique adventure. Their support and openness enabled a sense of excitement and joy to fill each day. May their journey be as rewarding and fulfilling.

Contents

ACKNOWLEDGEMENTS

Permission has been secured for quotes from the following sources:

Bonhoeffer, Dietrich, *Life Together.* Harper and Bros., New York. 1954.

Bonhoeffer, Dietrich, *Letters and Papers From Prison.* SCM Ltd., London.1953.

Bonhoeffer, Dietrich, *The Cost of Discipleship.* SCM Ltd., London. 1959.

East Asia Hymnal. East Asia Christian Conference, 1964.

Borg, Marcus J. *Meeting Jesus for the First Time.* Harper Collins, New York. 1995.

Ornish, Dean, *Love and Survival.* Harper Collins Publisher, New York. 1998.

Susuki, Daisetz T/, "The Role of Zen in Buddhism" in Olga Fröbc Kapteyn. ed. *Eranos-Jahrbuch,* (Zurich: Rhein-Verlag, 1954)

Keirsey, David, PLEASE UNDERSTAND ME, p.1, Copyright PNB Book Co. P.O. Box 2748,Delmar, CA 92014. Nemesis Books Co., Del Mar, CA. 1978.

Phillips, D. B., *The Choice Is Always Ours.* Harper and Row, New York. 1960.

Pelgrim, Mark, *And A Time To Die.* Edited by Sheila Moon and Elizabeth B. Howes. Routledge and Kegan Paul, London. 1961.

Murray, J. Middleton, *Jesus Man of Genius.* Harper and Bros, London and New York. 1926. Society of Authors Literary Representative of the Estate of John Middleton Murray.

Copyright 2004 James R. Hipkins

An Invitation

As we begin this journey, I want to introduce you to a person I have never met, though I feel I know him intimately. Dietrich Bonhoeffer has been one of the sources of strength and faith in my journey. It is amazing to realize that one can become so personally acquainted with someone through his books. I feel that I can carry on a conversation with him as I would with any of my close friends. His writings have become so much a part of my life that it is hard to distinguish at times what I have gleaned from him over the years.

Bonhoeffer was born in Breslau, Germany, in 1906, into a family of seven children. He grew up in Berlin, where his father, a noted physician, was the first to fill a chair of psychiatry in Germany. *"From his father, as he wrote in his last letter from prison, he learned, what characterizes all that he wrote, an insistent realism, a "turning away from the phraseological to the real." For him Christianity could never be merely intellectual theory, doctrine divorced from life, or mystical emotion, but always it must be responsible, obedient action, the discipleship of Christ in every situation of concrete everyday life, personal and public."*[1] It was this that ultimately led in the end to prison and death. Six years before his imprisonment by the Gestapo, he had written, "When Christ calls a man, he bids him come and die."

There are many excellent books written about and by Bonhoeffer. I would urge you to read them and become more intimately acquainted with this unique individual. I want to just look at the broad outline of his life so that the reader can become acquainted with one of the most fearless leaders in the twentieth century.

When Hitler came to power in Germany, Bonhoeffer was teaching in England. He returned to Germany in 1935 to share in the life and struggle of his people. He received a call from the Confessing Church in Germany to return home in order to lead an emergency Seminary in Pomerania for training ministers. His influence was the greatest in the witness he made through his writing. He wrote tracts against compromise in the Church struggle. In this era, *The Cost of Discipleship* was written (1937), as well as *Life Together* (1938), the two books

1. Bonhoeffer, Dietrich, *Life Together*, Harper Brothers, New York, 1954, p.8.

that had so much impact on my life and thought. They are the two most widely known books he wrote.

As a participant in the resistance in Germany and one of those who developed the plan to assassinate Hitler, Bonhoeffer was a marked man. On April 5, 1943 he was arrested by the Gestapo and was placed in the Tegel Prison in Berlin until October 8, 1944. After the failed attempt on Hitler's life, he was transferred from one prison to another and finally Flossenburg. He was on the list of those who must not survive the last days of the Third Reich. On April 9, 1945, he was executed at Flossenburg.

I first encountered Bonhoeffer in articles in the magazine *Intercollegian,* published by the Student Christian Movement during my days at Ohio Wesleyan. When I went to theological school at Boston, I had the opportunity to begin to read some of the books in the library. From the very first, the authenticity of his words sounded clearly through the pages. Bonhoeffer confronted me with challenges of commitment I had never anticipated. When I read *Letters and Papers from Prison,* I was brought to a point of commitment in my life that was summarized by Bonhoeffer when he wrote, "When Christ calls a man he bids him come and die." Commitment is not a polite agreement to study and understand. Rather, it is a turning over to God one's total being and allowing God to use one as God chooses. Bonhoeffer wrote a poem while in prison that expresses this in simple and very human terms.

WHO AM I?[2]

Who am I? They often tell me
    I stepped from my cell's confinement
    Calmly, cheerfully, firmly,
    Like a squire from his country-house.
Who am I? They often tell me
    I used to speak to my warders
Freely and friendly and clearly,
As though it were mine to command.
Who am I? They also tell me
I bore the days of misfortune

2. Bonhoeffer, D. *Letters and Papers from Prison*, SCM Press, London. 1953. p.165.

Equably, smilingly, proudly,
Like one accustomed to win.

Am I then really all that which other men tell of?
Or am I only what I myself know of myself?
Restless and longing and sick, like a bird in a cage,
Struggling for breath, as though hands were compressing my throat,
Yearning for colors, for flowers, for the voices of birds,
Thirsting for words of kindness, for neighborliness,
Tossing in expectation of great events,
Powerlessly trembling for friends at an infinite distance,
Weary and empty at praying, at thinking, at making,
Faint, and ready to say farewell to it all?

Who am I? This or the other?
Am I one-person to-day and to-morrow another?
Am I both at once? A hypocrite before others,
And before myself a contemptible woebegone weakling?
Or is something within me still like a beaten army,
Fleeing in disorder from victory already achieved?

Who am I? They mock me, these lonely questions of mine.
Whoever I am, Thou knowest, O God, I am Thine!

I want to share with you the books by Bonhoeffer, which have accompanied me through fifty years of discipleship. They will give you some idea of what influence he has had on my life. You will find through out my book the streams of his influence entering into the main current of my life.

Dietrich Bonhoeffer, *The Cost of Discipleship*, SCM Press, London, 1954. 273 pp.

Dietrich Bonhoeffer, *Life Together,* Harper & Bros., New York, 1954. 122 pp.

Dietrich Bonhoeffer, *Letters and Papers from Prison*, SCM Press Ltd., London, 1953. 201pp.

Dietrich Bonhoeffer, *Act and Being,* Collins, London, 1956. 184pp.

Heinrich Ott, *Reality and Faith: Theological Legacy of Dietrich Bonhoeffer, Fortress Press*, Philadelphia. 1972. 451pp.

Dietrich Bonhoeffer, *No Rusty Swords,* Edited by Edwin H. Robertson, Collins, London, 1965. 372pp..

Dietrich Bonhoeffer, *Creation and Fall,* SCM Press, London, 1959. 96pp.

Dietrich Bonhoeffer, *Spiritual Care,* Fortress Press, Philadelphia. 1985. 89pp.

Dietrich Bonhoeffer, *Ethics,* Edited by Eberhard Bethge. Collins, London, 1964.372pp.

Dietrich Bonhoeffer, *Sanctorum Communio,* Collins, London. 1963. (Doctoral Dissertation.)

A SPECIAL NOTE IN REGARDS TO THE USE OF THE WORD "CHINESE"

Throughout the book is talk about the "Chinese". When I use this term it refers specifically to the Chinese people who were and are living in Sarawak, East Malaysia. I use the term to refer to the Foochows, which are a very distinct language group from Fukien Province in China. You cannot generalize about all the Chinese throughout the world from my discussion. The observations are from one exclusive group of Chinese. I caution the reader to keep this in mind he journeys through the book.

1

A Terrifying Encounter

As rivers have their source in some far off fountain, so the human spirit has its source. To find his fountain of spirit is to learn the secret of heaven and earth.

—Laotzu, sixth century B. C., Chinese philosopher

The wind was bitter. It chilled me to the bone. There were no stars or moon. Standing in the eerie darkness, every now and then, I heard a sound. Was it a Russian, or an animal? It was my first night on guard at the mark on the road where we met the Russian Army. Ten feet away, the Russian guard stood motionless. I wanted a smoke but we were to use no matches. I began to pace back and forth across the narrow road. Five steps, turn, five steps back. I listened again. Nothing!

I was on duty at what was later the infamous CheckPoint Charley where a wall separated East Germany from West Germany. The outpost was about 800 yards outside of Rasdorf, Germany, the exact spot where we had met the Russian Army as they pushed toward Frankfort. Here they had stopped and so did we, the Americans.

As I walked guard duty, every sound seemed ominous. The slightest breeze made a noise in the nearest tree. But I continued back and forth. I remember, I should put on my bayonet. I forgot to do it when they dropped me off. I stopped, took the bayonet out of its holder and clicked it to my M1. I slung the rifle over my shoulder and continued to pace. I checked to make sure I had a clip of bullets in my rifle. I was dying for a smoke. I remembered one of the guys had given me a little chewing tobacco. I put some in my mouth and started to chew and pace. It did help; I couldn't feel the cold anymore. I was scared. Only the Russian soldier on his side and me on our side. Whew! I was really scared. I stopped walking for a few moments and I thought about life back home in Ohio.

I saw myself sitting on our side porch in Leipsic on a brown wicker swing. It held three of us, my dad, mom and me, as we swung in the early evenings in the spring and summer. There was a matching wicker chair and a wicker end table. Spirea bushes filled the air.

As my mother and I sat shelling peas, snapping beans, or pitting cherries, or pealing apples or just talking, life unfolded in Leipsic. Sometimes my dad shared in our conversations in the evening.

Here in this lonely outpost in Germany I felt the warmth of my family so far away. I could feel myself standing next to my mother, gentle, thoughtful and ever sensitive to my presence. She talked about the roses and their beauty, the flowers in the rock garden, the trip we were planning to make to Columbus Grove to visit and swim.

That night on duty in Germany, I traveled in my mind and dreamed. Time and again I would tour the world. Now here I was four thousand miles from home, in the middle of Germany on guard duty tonight. I remembered my father reading to me. I was four, frustrated by not being able to read. Little did we understand how much this moment was to determine the direction of my life.

2

Preparation for the Journey

It is with a sense of enormous relief and reassurance, our Father, that we come into Thy presence with our lives as they are, confident that Thou understands us and deals with each of us in accordance with our needs[1]*.*

In 1943, the call of the future asserted itself in my life. That year, I attended the Methodist Youth Institute at Lakeside, Ohio. Speaker after speaker lifted up the challenge of the future in the brave witness of many from our communities who were serving in the military. The Dean led us in a consecration service at the Institute. I responded to the challenge to turn my life over to God and allow Him to use me. Something was beckoning me to the altar that night. We received a card to indicate our commitment. I pledged myself to full-time Christian service. I had no idea what it meant, but I believed that God would reveal that to me. I remember leaving South Auditorium filled with emotion. I noticed no one. I merged with the crowd of youth as we made our way slowly to the lake carrying our lit candles. Every step led to more thought of what a commitment meant for my life. As I sat on the lakeshore that evening, I was overwhelmed with the thought that I had to find a way to involve myself in the War. It was as though God was focusing the direction of my life.

For the next two years, I was haunted by that commitment I had made at Lakeside. In the summer of 1944, I learned about a program called the Army Special Training Program that provided an opportunity for young men to join the Army and attend a university. I talked to my parents about applying. They said I had to finish my senior year, however, perhaps something could be worked out since my father was the clerk of the school board. He asked at the next meeting about what would be entailed if a student enrolled in the ASTP program.

---

1. Church Bulletin Meditation, Mt. Washington United Methodist Church, Cincinnati, OH, 1990 by the author.

The school administration said that if the student was accepted, they would count that the equivalent of the senior year, and would give the student a diploma next May.

I was accepted by the ASTP and was ordered to report to the induction center in Toledo, the first of August, 1944. I passed everything and was sworn into the Army at that time, and was assigned to the ASTP unit at Ohio State.

I was the only student who had not finished high school. We were enrolled in a program of math and science that far eclipsed anything at Leipsic High School. I managed to pass most of the subjects. Although I was fascinated by the classes in physics and some of the math, much of the other material I never did grasp. When the first semester was about half finished I went to see the First Sergeant. I told him that I had enlisted and was anxious to get into the thick of things. A number of good friends in Leipsic had been killed and I could not stand by and just study a book. I wanted to get into the action so I submitted a request for transfer to active duty with the Army. It was granted within a week. At the end of that semester, I was to report to basic training at Camp Wheeler in Macon, GA.

The six weeks training at Camp Wheeler were exciting. One felt that he was being prepared to defend the nation and to repel our enemies. When the Battle of the Bulge began in Europe, we had just started to go to the rifle range. Planes were flown in and parked near our training area. The rumor was going around that we might be shipped out soon. Needless to say the truth of the whole experience began to impact us. This is a war and we are in it!

Fortunately, we completed basic training, had a short, seven-day furlough home, and we were to report for transport to New York. There we were loaded aboard the troop ships. Previously, the ships had been escorted by the Navy because of the German submarine threat in the Atlantic, but when our convoy left New York, it was on its own. We had no idea what an unescorted convoy would mean in the North Atlantic. We didn't see any subs nor did we have any incidents. By this time, the Allies had driven the Germans back enough that their naval fleet no longer presented any kind of danger to shipping.

One night, our ship sailed into the harbor at Le Harve, France. This was our first glimpse of war and its aftermath. The harbor was filled with ships that had been sunk by the Allies. In fact, the troop ships had to proceed very slowly because of the congestion caused by the sunken ships. When we marched off the ship, it was damp and cold. Mud was everywhere. We were directed to tents that were at the peak of a small hill not far from the harbor. Occasionally, one would hear the sound of artillery. As we went into our tents, we put our gear on a bed and sat down to take stalk of where we were. I looked up and saw that the top of tent looked like a sieve with holes everywhere. Foolishly, I asked what was the matter with it, and was quickly informed they were bullet holes. I didn't say another word. I recall sleeping very lightly that night. Before dawn, at 5 a.m., I was awakened and told to bring my gear because we were shipping out. Breakfast would be just before we boarded the trains.

There must have been at least fifty of us loaded into a boxcar, with K Rations(a box containing our food rations for the trip.). In the center of the box car, sat a small pot bellied stove on which we could warm K rations.

As the train began to move, the doors were closed. As we began to roll, someone pointed out that the outhouse was in the corner. It was a bucket; its odor would etch itself forever into my memory. After several hours the train stopped. We slid the door back to see where we were and to air out the car. There was a strange looking railroad station. We could not read the writing, since none of us could read any European language. One of our group saw somebody and tried to ask where we were, and the reply came back, "Belgium." The next 24 hours we moved steadily forward. We had no idea where we were going or what was happening outside. Occasionally, we stopped and they let us get out for a quick smoke and to stretch our legs. It must have been at least two days before the train finally stopped, and we were told to bring our gear and line up. There were a number of 2½-ton trucks to transport us to an unknown destination. The trucks roared out of the railroad area heading in different directions. About three or four trucks followed our truck.

When they stopped, we got out and lined up. We were assigned to this or that platoon and we left. That evening we gathered in a small room with the Colonel. The Colonel was the commander of the 7th Regiment of the 3rd Infantry Division. He welcomed us to the division and to the Regiment. He then told us some of the heroic history of the unit to which we had been assigned. From the Cotton Bales of New Orleans, the 7th Infantry Regiment had gotten its name "the Cotton Balers" while they were under the command of Andrew Jackson. They had fought from the shores of North Africa, to Italy, then to Germany. We joined them for the final thrust to destroy Germany and the Axis powers. After the pep rally, we were ready to go into the battle with our new comrades.

We had no idea of the future or what we were to do. I was to discover quickly that my responsibility was to remove mines and booby traps so the troops could come into villages and areas quickly. We were to do our jobs silently, efficiently and effectively. There were fifty men in the company when we arrived. We were designated the ANTI-TANK Co. of the 7th Regiment. We had bazookas and 57mm guns, but our major task was removing mines. The troops were moving so fast that we would not worry about tanks. In fact, we seldom, if ever, used our rifles or carbines. Knives were our most effective weapons. Usually we were so close to the Germans that the fire of arms would have alerted them to our positions.

In twelve months I had gone from Leipsic, Ohio and high school to southern Germany. I was paralyzed with fear. I had no idea of our location. As the Allies pushed north, the Germans began to mine more areas, and we worked night and day taking up mines and freeing the roads and paths so we could keep the Germans on the run. In many cases we were taking up the mines almost as fast as they were laying them. Very often we would come up on a group of three or four Germans just as they finished laying mines, and as they were just about to leave, we would sneak up and surprise them with our drawn knives. We dared not shoot because the Germans were only several hundred yards from our position.

We were fortunate that we always were able to have a one-on-one situation. We always had a sufficient number to enable us to move in silently for the kill. I only took part in three or four such events, but that was more than enough.

We went quickly through the German towns. They seemed very small and close together. Stuttgart was the biggest city we encountered, but we were told to get through it as fast as possible and begin to clear the paths beyond. It seemed like a feverish pitch. Often, we slept only an hour or so and then were on the go again. A barn was utilized as the billet for a few hours of sleep and then it was on to the next stop. We had come about half way up in Germany, and we found ourselves on the outskirts of a small village called Rasdorf. We approached carefully but found it quiet. We gathered in the village square and the company commander ordered several squads to fan out to the borders of the town. Just as we got to the edge of town, trucks were roaring down the road. They were not American. As they got closer we saw them—Russian trucks. We had met up with the Russians. The war was now over. The truce had been signed and we were to settle into Rasdorf and wait for further orders.

We set up our guard post next to the Russian guard just outside the town. The Russians put up a bunkhouse for those who would man this post. At the end of the war, a big party was planned with the Russians. Americans were to bring the whisky and they, the vodka. It was quite a night of singing and shouting. They would sing and then we would sing. They would sing and dance and then we would sing and dance. By dawn everything in Rasdorf was quiet.

We were billeted in a farm home. The German family had to provide a room in which four of us were to sleep. I recall walking through their kitchen each morning as they were having breakfast; no one spoke or smiled. The German family sat with their heads down as if in mourning as we passed by. Sometimes a young person would raise his eyes just enough to see us going by.

We were there for a week. Our supply sergeant was busy going to some town to get beer each day. About the third day, two squads went to a refugee camp several miles away. The refugees were arriving in huge numbers, but before they could enter the camp, they had to be searched; that was our job. The refugees came with suitcases, boxes, bags, cloth bags, and small cases containing all of their possessions. One woman had a large suitcase in which she had only cutlery. She had been carrying it all over Europe since fleeing Poland. During lunch break on our first day, several of us went for a short walk outside the camp. Suprise! We discovered a German ammunition bunker filled with shells and grenades. The company commander was called; he immediately set in motion actions to remove all the ammunition and other weapons in the cache.

In the early evening, we returned to Rasdorf. When we arrived at breakfast the next morning we were informed that some of the Polish refugees had killed several Germans as they were walking on the road near the camp. Also, several farms had been set on fire last night. We were going to be assigned to guard a German farm family for one or two days, until all the Polish refugees were rounded up. Four of us were assigned to a German farm home comfortably furnished. The people were very appreciative and friendly. The mother had baked some pastry for us to enjoy with coffee. Each of us took a window on each of the four sides of the home. We stayed up all night, going outside occasionally to see if there was any movement. There were no incidents that night. The next night, we returned for the same duty. Nothing happened. The third morning, new orders came for our company. We were ordered to go to Zigenheim to take over Stalag 95. It was a prison camp filled with Wehrmacht and Luftwaffe prisioners. By late morning we were ready to pull out of Rasdorf and arrived at Zigenheim by early afternoon. Interestingly, as soon as we pulled out, the Russians moved into town. However, during the cold war, Rasdorf was to be in West Germany. Sometime later the Russians moved back to the place where we met them.

Zigenheim was a very different experience. We knew absolutely nothing about running a prison camp. I assume there were those who did, but our responsibility was guard duty at the front gate and in the towers that surrounded the camp.

I would estimate that we had close to 500 German prisoners. Most were not actually foot soldiers. Each of us had a private room where we slept. Three of us shared a small sitting room and in the center of that room was a small heating stove. Our room was cleaned by a prisoner who had been the President of the Bank of Germany. He had a good command of English but spoke only when spoken to. Each morning, he would build our fire and put on a pan of water so we could shave. We had no set time to get up. We could eat breakfast between 7:30 and 9 a.m. The most memorable part of our experience was the food at the camp. German cooks and bakers prepared our food so the Army cooks got some time off. The bakers were from Vienna. We had delicious rolls and pastries for breakfast. Also, a string quintet played for every meal. The string players had been in the Stuttgart Symphony Orchestra.

Guard duty was relatively easy, except for the front gate. We were in enclosed towers that were heated by a small, wood burning stove. A prisoner who had been a professor of agriculture at Heidelberg University tended the stove. At the front gate you stood guard outside and waited for people or vehicles to approach. It was uncomfortable to be posted at the front gate because there was a constant parade of families who walked on the road along the front of the camp. They walked from one end to the other, turned around and walked back, looking constantly to see if their loved one was here.

It was early Fall when we arrived in Zigenheim and we stayed until January. It was cold. The rains were heavy in October. One morning as the first sergeant was posting the guard, the vehicle, (a weasel that hauled seven or eight) almost got stuck in the mire. He slid around for about five minutes. Someone noticed something at the edge of the mud. A close examination revealed that it was a body—the body of an American soldier who had been buried in this spot. That afternoon a detail was taken back to the spot to dig. They uncovered a mass grave of American POW's who had either been killed or died. It took a week or so to clean up the grave. Several more were found outside the perimeter of the camp.

One day at camp in early December, we were walking by an empty building, or so we thought. We tried the door and forced it open. We entered and discovered a complete dark room for developing film and printing pictures. All the chemicals and equipment were there to be utilized. In high school, Bob Blume and I had developed pictures. I asked the first sergeant for permission to use the equipment. I assured him I knew how to use it. With his permission, I began to develop film for the company. Everyone brought film. Several wanted enlargements to send home for Christmas. My business got so busy that they released me from guard duty so I could spend 10-12 hours a day in the dark room. It was fun and certainly better than pulling guard duty.

In early January, they began to ship more prisoners to us by train. A train spur was just outside the camp about ½ mile away. We would meet the trains, unload the prisoners, and load them into trucks and we proceeded to Stalag 95. Some men from the American Army intelligence came to our camp and were busy interrogating the incoming prisoners. Most of the incoming Germans had been in Hitler's elite SS troops. At this point we were told that we would be relieved of our duty at the camp and were to move to Bad Salzschlirf. A Polish company replaced us. Where they were coming from I have no idea. They took over and we left. We did hear the next day that they had shot a whole carload of prisoners without even opening the doors. This was to occur several times before they understood it was unacceptable to the Allies.

One incident needs to be recorded, it happened when we were running the prison camp. Just before we left the camp, a number of the prisoners were transferred to Darmstadt. I was one of the guards to ride in trucks to the train station to oversee the transfer of the prisoners to the prison train. We were to ride the train to Darmstadt. As we went into town with large 2 ½ ton trucks, each with 25-30 German prisoners, the response of the public was interesting. As we drove through the town, people tossed bread, candy, wine, etc. to the men in the trucks. What should we do? We did nothing. When we got to the train station, hundreds of civilians were waiting. Many people wanted to see if their fathers, brothers, husbands or sons were among this group. Could they at least say hello and touch them? This question was evident on their faces. Our company formed a solid line on each side of the prisoners, with our weapons cocked and loaded. On several occasions I can recall allowing a woman to reach across and grab the prisoner who was going by and give him a kiss. It was really a touching but pathetic scene. The officers insisted we had to stop all human contact; we reluctantly complied. When we arrived at Darmstadt, we were shocked. There was no town! We loaded the prisoners onto a truck and rode with them to their new camp several miles away.

Piles of rubble were pushed into large heaps along the road. We saw no buildings standing. I cannot recall how we returned to Zigenheim, but after this transfer we then left for Bad Salzschlirf.

In Bad Salzschlirf, we were billeted in a hotel. It was a beautiful town. In fact, the town was mostly hotels. We were to discover that German amputees of one type or another were patients in most of the hotels. The hotels had been converted by the German Army into hospitals for amputees. We were not warmly welcomed. As we walked along the streets they would try to cut us with knives and poke us with sharp objects.

Jim Hipkins at Stalag 95 in 1946. Zigenheim, Germany

Cannon Company was also assigned to the town. Their hotel was a spa. This community was a resort of spas. We were allowed to use the spa at Cannon Company when we were in the mood. Our nights were spent raiding homes and apartments. The men in our company who had venereal disease were assigned to a special section of the dining room. At one point, almost half of our company were assigned to that area. I was promoted to company clerk as soon as we arrived at Bad Salzschlirf. I was the only person who could type. It was to be an interesting interlude for me. When the company went out to drill and exercise, I was in the office preparing reports.

I recall a First Lt. who was one of our officers at Rasdorf. When he returned to Rasdorf the next day to get his girl friend, he could not get into town because the Russian line had moved west of Rasdorf by this time.

In Bad Salzschlirf, there were many women who were becoming related to our company. Some of the non-coms, as well as some of the officers, had mistresses. I recall having to find one of the sergeants who was needed at the office. He was with his girl. Where did she live? We finally went to the Burgermeister's office to get help. He did tell us where she was living, and we got the Sergeant to the place where he needed to be.

When we had time off we would go into the enlisted men's club. Two weeks after we arrived we got the dubious title, the "VD Raiders of the 7th". Twenty-five to thirty men had contracted venereal disease since we left Rasdorf. So the Colonel decided that our company would have the honor of rounding up all the prostitutes and other persons who were shacking up at night in the area. Every night at 10 or 11 P.M., thirty of us were assigned to this duty. We would go down the streets of the assigned town and stop at every home and apartment building, go into every bedroom and look at passes. If the Germans had no pass for the area, they were to be rounded up and escorted to an area for relocation. It was terrible routing people out of bed in the middle of the night and forcing them to leave if they did not have the proper papers.

This was to be our last assignment in Germany. We had been there about two or three months. A dress parade and lowering of the colors was to be our last formal gathering as a company. The next day orders came for most of the company to return home. Several of us were assigned to Hershfeld, to be responsible for formally sending the entire company and records back to the U.S. The First Sergeant and I were given this responsibility.

The night before everyone left, one of the guys got drunk. He had a wife and three kids at home. He was anxious to get home, but he was worried about leaving his female German friend. The first Sergeant came in to inform him that he ought to go back and go to bed. He had had too much to drink. Unfortunately, he didn't like what was said. The first sergeant moved in closer and put his face in front of the other guy to let him know who was in charge. He did it several more times, and the guy swung a right to the sergeant. The first sergeant also had had a bit to drink and he informed the guy he wasn't going home tomorrow. In fact, he was going to place charges against him to have him court martialed.

I spent the next two days typing up the court-martial papers. In the midst of the preparations, we were notified that the company was to leave for home the next day.

Everyone began preparations to leave. The first sergeant and I were to go to Hersfeld to do the final preparations for the court martial and the final details on sending the company home. The soldier under arrest was to be transferred to Hersfeld for the trial. Several days after we arrived in Hersfeld, the trial was held. I was the main witness for the defense. Actually, I was the only witness because everyone else had left. The soldier was acquitted and sent home. Several days later the orders came through that I was to join a group of about 800 who were being transferred to Italy. We were the final remnants of the 3rd Division in Europe.

The next morning, we were assembled at Kassel and put aboard a train bound for somewhere in Italy.

When our train left Kassel it was early morning. We were given a keg of beer for each car. This time we were not in boxcars, but regular passenger cars. It was a most enjoyable ride. Soon we were pulling into a large rail terminal. The train came to stop. We would spend the night here. It turned out this was Stuttgart. Not one pane of glass was left in any window of that station. The entire station had originally been enclosed with a glass canopy. We left the next morning and proceeded to tour, so it seemed, most of southern Germany. The train chugged all night, and as the dawn broke it was evident that we were in the mountains. In fact we were going through the Brenner Pass. At about 9 A. M., the train stopped at the edge of small, rural town. We were told there was a stream just several hundred yards away where we could get out to wash and refresh ourselves. We ran to it, it was cold, clear, and flowing rapidly. It was from the melting snow on the mountaintop. We splashed our faces, brushed our teeth, had time for a K Ration, and were off. We spent another night on the train and when morning came, we were ordered to remove all our gear and assemble outside. We were transported to a large building where we were to be living. Actually, it was probably around 3 or 4 in the morning when we arrived. We were given a room and most of us went immediately to sleep. In what seemed to be only a few hours, a bugle sounded. We got up and fell out into a formation of sorts, in the open area between two buildings. We were informed that we were now assigned to the 88th Division, 346 Infantry Regiment.

As the officers of the 88th Division walked down the ranks informing us, it was evident that most of the 800 were non-commissioned officers. They taunted us a bit that we were no longer in the 3rd Division. But strangely, within two months every major position in that regiment was held by a former 3rd Division, non-com. This experience happened in every company and in every regiment. I was immediately assigned as the company clerk.

Several weeks later our company was directed to prepare to move to the Morgan Line. This was the line drawn between Italy and Yugoslavia that controlled the disputed city of Trieste. We had received word that the Russian Army had moved in on the other side of the mountain and appeared likely to be preparing to move across the Morgan Line. The Allies were committed to preserve this line. We arrived on the Morgan Line at Outpost 36. Our company headquarters was a former inn located at this spot. We were to be responsible for at least two other outposts on the line. No one was to cross the line. There was a gate across the road and we were on one side and Yugoslavs were on the other. Each guard was about 10 feet from the other. There were some persons going back and forth across the line each day. Most of the people were farmers who had to go to their fields.

Although I was the company clerk, on several occasions, I had to go on patrol. We were assigned on a regular basis. One outpost was about three miles from our headquarters. I was to go on this patrol. We would begin at about nine in the evening. It would take about an hour to get to the outpost and we would spend a while there. We would return about 11 p.m. It was a lonely walk with six men on the patrol. No talking, just walking and listening. Our concern was the telephone line that linked the outpost to headquarters. It was cut almost daily. The first time I went on patrol I was scared. When we began our patrol, we had about 20 to 30 feet between us. We went slowly but carefully. As we got further away from the headquarters, the road was lined with thick woods on both sides. The road was just an old, dirt road that only a jeep could navigate. I recall vividly seeing something in the dark. It was still, but was in the shape of man. He was kneeling. It was as if he appeared to be waiting for us to pass. I stopped, cocked my gun. I stood looking at the object. The soldier behind me came up to see what was the matter. He stood there looking. I whispered to him, "What do you think?" He said he couldn't tell. We both stood there silently for what seemed to be an hour, but I am sure was just some seconds. Finally, I said, "Who goes there?" There was only silence. No reply! I repeated my challenge! Nothing! We opened fire, and I must have emptied a whole clip into the unknown intruder. We crept forward carefully, and discovered that we had shredded an old stump. We went on without incident.

This outpost was to be an important site in several weeks. As the weeks passed, some were assigned to the outpost where we had gone on the previous week. I was assigned with the group. One night after everyone was in bed, a hand grenade went off. Then another and another—one after another. It was obvious it was not one of ours. Had the Russians decided now was the time to cross the Morgan line? Silence! We listened. It seemed our ears were more sensitive than ever before. Every little sound was magnified. We stayed up the rest of the night on alert. We were never informed whether the grenades were thrown by the Russians or the Yugoslavs.

Outpost 35 on the Morgan Line in 1946.

The Russians had at least 40,000 troops on the other side of the mountain from us. We had 150 men. Hardly any contest at all. It would have been a sheer massacre if they had begun anything of a serious nature. The tension would remain high along the Morgan Line for the foreseeable future. All of us were edgy. It began to tell in a number of ways. In town, the fights between Americans and British troops were on the increase. It got so bad that we had a series of friendly exchanges with British non-coms coming to our companies, and some of our non-com's going to their companies for at least 3 or 4 days. It was to this checkpoint, Outpost 36, that bodies of the six American pilots who were shot down over Yugoslavia were brought back to the Allies. They were reconnaissance pilots. It was a big international incident when it happened. It brought us to the brink of war. Diplomacy apparently worked, and things began to get calm.

I was discharged from the Army in April, 1947, after having been in Europe for two years. About eight months before my discharge, I contracted a very serious case of pneumonia and was hospitalized for two weeks. My recuperation seemed normal, but by the time I arrived in the States and was discharged, I had a persistent cough. Not only was it persistent, but I had begun to ache in my ribcage when I coughed. At the time, my father worked for the Veterans' Administration in Toledo, Ohio and insisted that I see a VA doctor. Reluctantly, I went for a physical exam.

In the meantime, I was ready to get back into civilian life. Since I had worked for the Kroger Grocery Company prior to entering the Army, I went to the District office in Toledo and whom should I encounter but the man who had been the District Manager prior to my military experience. He knew me quite well. He asked, "What are you doing here?" "I'm looking for a job," I replied.

He said, "Look no further. I have an opening at a store on the eastside of Toledo and you would be perfect for it. I'll see you there tomorrow at 9 A.M."

I was riding high at that point. I met him the next day and was employed as the assistant manager of the store. Within one week, I had a call from the VA doctor. The next day, I went to see him and he informed me that I had a serious problem with my lungs. He was not sure what the prognosis was at this point; however, he advised me immediately to quit work and come for further examinations. I felt as if someone had hit me in the stomach and sent me into the ropes. The next weeks were filled with anxiety. The doctors wanted to place me in the VA Tuberculosis Hospital in Minnesota. My father said, "No! You don't have TB." The doctors worked out a series of treatments using ultraviolet ray lamps and giving me penicillin by mouth. The next two months were filled with continuing medical attention.

Between treatments, I found myself sitting at home. I was so depressed that I could hardly move. What was I going to do? How long would I have to sit around and do nothing?

In my confusion, I decided to apply to a college, since I could do nothing else. I didn't expect to be accepted but it would give me something to pass my time. I filled out two applications for Ohio Wesleyan University and Miami University of Ohio.

In the meantime, I still had the summer with nothing to do. I remembered that Doc Miller had his office in Toledo. He was the camp director of the Toledo YMCA camp which I attended as a young boy. As I entered his office, he stood up and rapidly moved across the room to shake my hand. He called me by name. He wanted to know all about what had been happening in my life. He mentioned a job opening at camp. In fact, he said, "The job is just made for you. I want you to take charge of the rifle ranges for the summer." I replied, "That sounds great!"

Before my summer employment began, I received a reply from Ohio Wesleyan University. They were sorry that I had applied so late, but they would be happy to put me on the list for 1948. For some reason, that made me angry. My Mom, my grandfather, an uncle, and a cousin had attended Ohio Wesleyan. I got in the car and drove to Leipsic, Ohio, to see Earl Edwards who had been one of my teachers in high school and who attended the Methodist Church in which I grew up. His family had donated the gymnasium to Ohio Wesleyan. I asked him if he could write me a letter that would speed up my entrance to OWU. He took half a sheet of paper, wrote several sentences on it and directed me to send it to the university admissions office at once. I did as directed. By return mail, I received a notice that OWU would welcome me to the campus in September, 1947. Enclosed were enrollment papers.

The summer camp was hard work, but fun. Most of all, I was able to swim. In fact, I hoped to try out for the college swimming team. At camp, I swam a quarter of a mile twice a day. My strokes were stronger and my pace was getting faster. I was fortunate that I was able to work at the camp that summer. I thought that I might even try out for the USA Olympic team.

By fall the VA had me on pills. I had a whole bag of medicine to take to college. When I arrived on campus, I was loaded with pills and my chest was in constant pain. I couldn't take a breath without discomfort. At the end of the first week on campus, I asked the university doctor to tape my chest so it could not expand. This reduced the pain.

During the first few weeks at college, I met the captain of the swimming team. He invited me to come to the initial tryouts at the campus pool. Swimming practice was fun. The major emphasis at the first practice was to swim 25 laps. I dove in and swam the allotted laps. I cannot recall finishing or showering. The only thing I remembered about the practice was that I woke up in my bed the next morning, but I didn't remember coming home. I asked the fellows with whom I lived, "Who brought me home?" They didn't recall that anybody brought me home. I spoke to the captain of the team, and he had no idea how I got home that evening. Apparently, I was in some kind of shock following the laps. I was scared. I thought about the experience and came to the conclusion that my swimming days were finished.

The next eight months of my first year at OWU were divided between the hospital and classes. The pain in my chest was often unbearable. When I got out of the hospital I went on drinking binges so that I could tolerate the pain. A week later, I was back in the hospital. Before the year ended, the doctors attempted to get me to drop out of college and rest. I refused. Miraculously I was able to finish the year.

3

To OWU, Boston, Ceylon, and India in Search of Answers

Many paths before us lie,
Many voices to us cry;
Which of all these shall we choose,
Here find gain or there all lose?
Jesus take our hands in Thine
Guide us by Thy grand design[1]

At the close of my first year at Ohio Wesleyan in May, 1948, a friend Matt and I were not doing very well in an introductory course to the Bible. Dr. Harold Hutson suggested that we would find tutoring helpful for the final examination. He said we should contact Matt's sister who graded the professor's tests. We arranged a tutoring session. When we arrived, we discovered that his sister had invited one of the other graders, Charlotte Wahl, to help her. After we finished the tutoring session, we discussed coming events. In the fall of 1948, Ohio Wesleyan was going to admit two black women. Some of the Young Women's Christian Association members had discussed inviting one of the students to be their roommate. Matt's sister, Chuckie Legge and Charlotte Wahl were involved in that effort. During the conversation we had a heated argument on inter-racial dating. Since I grew up in an all-white community, I had a very limited exposure to non-whites. I had met only one Negro in my life. During my time in the Army, the Army was segregated so there was no inter-racial contact. I had definite ideas that were not based on anything but prejudice. The prejudice was pure ignorance. The discussion ended; I was sure that the girls would never speak to us again.

1. East Asia Christian Council Hymnal, 1964, words by Y.L.Yang, no. 151.

Since the VA would not allow me to work the summer of 1948, I spent my time lounging around home and going to Lakeside-on Lake Erie to spend time at the family cottage. My aunt was open to my dropping in regularly. On July 4, 1948, an important event occurred. My family gathered at Lakeside to celebrate the holiday. My uncle, George Kibler and I went to take a walk and look at the girls. He loved to look and so did I. George and I were sitting on a bench in front of the hotel watching all the young women on their way to swim or sunbathe. One young woman walked by and my uncle said, "Wow, look at those legs." I thought I recognized her. It was Charlotte Wahl from college. Our last meeting had been memorable because of the intense discussion we had had about race. I said, "Hello!" She was courteous but aloof. Several days later, I met a friend from Findlay, Ohio, who had come to Lakeside. He suggested finding a couple of girls to go to Cedar Point Amusement Park the next day. That evening, he and I went to the hotel to eat and who was our waitress? It was Charlotte Wahl. Before we left I had arranged a date with her for the next evening. She promised to ask another waitress to come with my friend.

That was the beginning of the rest of my life. We make choices and decisions. Divine intervention, I doubt it. Hormones, perhaps. Regardless, Charlotte and I were together two or three times a week the rest of the summer. Our long walks and conversations led to exciting discussions of the future. I found myself beginning to emerge from my depression.

During 1948, I spent no time in the hospital. My chest pain returned with some severity at times, so I went to the doctor to get taped. The other problem that seemed to plague me was my leg which had been hurt during the war-shrapnel had injured the muscles in the left leg.

During the 1948–49 academic year Charlotte Wahl and I would spend most of our extra time at Ohio Wesleyan with each other. In December of 1948 I asked her to marry me. In August 1949 we were married. During this period I focused my energy on a career.

At the end of the 1950 academic year at Ohio Wesleyan, my wife and I needed summer employment. In March, an assistant director of The College Settlement of Philadelphia came to speak to my Urban Sociology class about their Farm Camp, an inter-racial and inter-faith camp. The camp needed counselors. Since it sounded challenging, I picked-up application blanks, applied and were accepted.

For the next four summers we would work at the College Settlement Farm Camp (the second year we were appointed the directors of the Mansion House, for 6-10 year olds). It was an inter-racial camp. Half of the staff and approximately fifty-percent the campers were non-white. I learned about discrimination at fast food places as well as the latent prejudice that seems to always lie just beneath the surface. By the end of our time at Farm Camp, I was feeling comfortable with Blacks We had a warm relationship as a staff. Some had a special role in my education. Earl Norris became a close friend. He was a young Afro-American man whose determination to finish high school inspite of constant stuttering, inspired me in my own journey. Jim Graves, a counselor, was the son of a Black Baptist minister in Philadelphia. His father invited me to come to services on Sunday, since I was studying for the ministry. I had never been to a Black home, let alone a Black church and I was afraid. I declined the invitation. Ever since I have been ashamed of my fear.

At the International Affairs Banquet at Ohio Wesleyan in the Spring of 1950, I had an unforgettable experience. Dr. Allan Knight Chalmers was the speaker for the evening. As the treasurer of the NAACP, he had led in the struggle to free the Scottsboro boys from prison, was one of the founders of the Fellowship of Reconciliation and a former pastor of Broadway Tabernacle in New York City. He was currently the Professor of Homiletics at Boston University, School of Theology. His speech was focused on how violence had played havoc with international relations and the fascination of humankind with violence. He inferred that WWII had been just another fatal attempt to correct evil with violence. As he spoke, I became angry. I became aware that I was forcing my fork to bend in half because of my anger. My wife was disturbed by my behavior. Chalmers continued passionately to make a persuasive appeal for pacifism and all its implications. My insides were churning. I was shaking visibly as we got up to leave after the benediction.

During my senior year at Ohio Wesleyan, I had conversations with professors about what would be appropriate for me to pursue as a profession. I had begun in pre-law and that seemed to be an option. My year as president of the campus YMCA exposed me to a type of work that I found exciting. Perhaps the pastoral ministry would be a place where my talents could be useful, or perhaps City Management was a new field that was promising for one with my background. Yet, in the back of my mind were comments that various persons had made about my goals in life. Doc Miller had commented at Camp Storer, in the summer of 1947 that I ought to think about the ministry. He had been impressed by the devotional services that I led at the Camp Storer. Professor Diem, our debate coach, said once that I had a voice that should be used. I had finished a second major in religion my senior year. I talked to Goldie McCue, a religion professor, about finding a meaningful life work. She also mentioned the ministry. I asked about where one should go to theological school if he decided that was the right direction. She said, "Look at the type of people who come from that school The school will determine what type of person you will be in the future. Choose it carefully." I shared this with Charlotte and spent several weeks wrestling with the decision. Finally, I decided that Boston University was the place where I wanted to prepare for the ministry.

In September, 1951, we were in Boston, matriculating at the School of Theology. As soon as we arrived, we were invited to attend a Young Friends Group at the Cambridge Society of Friends. The directors of Farm Camp in Philadelphia were Quakers. We looked forward to learning more about the Quakers. We were immediately swept up into the warm concern and determined effort that was evident in this group in facing the critical issues of the day. We found the discussions stimulating and challenging. I had never been in a group that thought in terms of non-violence. Equality was a given in all things. The first year, we became involved with the Young Friends Weekend Work Camps. By the end of the year, Charlotte and I were hired to direct the work camps during the 1951–52 academic year. For the next two years, we guided the Young Friends through the work camps in the inner city of Cambridge and Boston, confronting a large influx of refugees from Europe and the inevitable issues of race, poverty and crime.

Most of all we were learning the Quaker method. It was a unique way of leading groups that would introduce us to a new understanding of leadership. Although consensus is difficult for non-Friends to grasp and accept, I felt comfortable with it and came to understand that it is a very positive way to interact with people. The experience of leading groups using the Quaker style would establish the leadership model for my ministry. My understanding of poverty, crime and racial issues began to take me to places I never knew existed. I found myself exposed to a world that was far beyond the experience of someone from a small town in rural Ohio. From a limited experience, I emerged with a deep commitment to equality, and everything that was to emerge in the coming Civil Rights movement.

Boston University School of Theology exposed me to issues that revolutionized my life and my commitments. These were the years that Martin Luther King was also a student at Boston University School of Theology as well as a number of other Black young persons who would be leaders in the upcoming Civil Rights Movement. It was a unique time to be at Boston and involved with the emerging issues.

During the first week at Boston University, School of Theology, Dr. Henry Hitt Crane, from the Central Methodist Church in Detroit, preached two sermons at chapel. He first spoke on the topic of "Thermostats or Thermometers". He asked us in the sermon, "Did we wish to effect change in the world or merely register the temperature of the world?" In the afternoon he preached at 1 p.m. This sermon was even more gripping and he had my rapt attention. For three hours, he preached to an overflow crowd. No one left nor moved. I, too, was transfixed by his message of Love and Redemption. He spoke of Jesus' ethic of love and forgiveness, the root of reconciliation. When he finished, he led us in a prayer of commitment to a life of non-violence rooted in the love of Jesus Christ. Never had my heart been moved to the depths of this single experience. That evening, I related to Charlotte the commitment to non-violence I had made at the conclusion of Crane's sermon. This was a far cry from the young man at Ohio Wesleyan just three months ago who had vigorously lobbied to bring ROTC to the campus.

The professor of preaching at Boston University, School of Theology, was Allan Knight Chalmers. He was etched vividly in my mind after his speech at Ohio Wesleyan. All of my experiences at BU focused on the heart of one's commitment to Jesus Christ. From Henry Hitt Crane with his challenge of pacifism, Dr. Chalmers and his passion for justice and equality, Dean Muelder and his insistence on coherence in our ethics and theology, to the constant debate throughout the school, the radical nature of the call to discipleship was clear and could not be evaded.

These experiences brought insight and understanding to the direction of my life. I remember how at Ohio Wesleyan Harold Hutson in his courses on the Bible, challenged all of my old assumptions about life and the Bible. Also, Goldie McCue's class in the Teachings of Jesus at Ohio Wesleyan enabled me to be receptive to Chalmers, Crane, Walter Muelder, Harold DeWolf, Cliff Moore, Paul Johnson, Pat McConnell and a host of other teachers whom I would encounter at Boston. I have found the journey to be exciting, challenging, and at times disillusioning. The intellectual and spiritual resources which I acquired at the School of Theology would enable me to seek and discover answers to some of the most troubling questions in my journey. *Is there really meaning in life? What is worthwhile? In what should I invest my life? What goals are worthy of the life I have been given? Is money a worthy goal? Is success in whatever career I choose sufficient? What is success? Is it fame? Is it fortune? Is it acclaim? Is there really a power that is beyond human comprehension that moves and empowers life? Are there resources available that can enable a person to live inspite of the darkness?*

At this point in my life, I became aware of Dietrich Bonhoeffer. I discovered that he had been struggling with the questions which I had struggled with in recent weeks. What is required of one who commits himself to Christ? How does pacifism fit into one's life? In his book, *The Cost of Discipleship,* Dietrich Bonhoffer focused for me the beginning of the quest to understand the issues and the witness that must be made by Christians in our world. He said, "**Grace is not cheap.**" To accept Jesus Christ as the Center of one's life means that the authority in my life will be Jesus Christ. I give all I have to Him. He does not ask for a casual commitment to a creed or the Kingdom of God, he asks for my life.

In 1957, I found myself wrestling with the meaning of my commitment to Jesus Christ. I certainly had given my life to Him and to His Church. Was I not ordained? I did everything that was expected of a pastor and a Christian. I had no reason to feel uncomfortable in my heart. Yet there was growing restlessness in my life. It didn't make sense. I was appointed to establish and develop a new church in a very affluent area of Cincinnati. Everything was far ahead of schedule. By the second year the new community of faith was self-supporting. New members were joining our congregation every week. Enthusiasm was high. We were developing a new church similar to Church of the Saviour in Washington, D.C. In 1958, I went to Washington, D.C. to a seminar at Church of The Saviour for clergy to discover ways of enabling a community of faith to develop in this new area.

One of the central insights from the seminar that we adopted in the new congregation in Cincinnati was that God calls individuals to discipleship. We do not invite others to join the church; Jesus Christ invites them. It is His church. Therefore, our way of visiting in the homes of people in the community took a very different focus. We were sharing an invitation to join in our adventure to understand what it means to be God's people in this community. We offered invitations to come and share in our experiences and encounters with Jesus Christ. It was interesting to see what happened. People attended for several months and then they would approach me and ask why no one invited them to join the church? I explained that I did not invite people to join; Jesus Christ invites persons to become a part of His community. I explained that if they felt Christ had brought them to this place and wanted them to join, they could indicate that to me and we would welcome them into our membership classes and into our fellowship. This conviction etched itself deeply into the life of the new congregation.

By the third year, I was uneasy at the speed with which people were joining our church. I received a copy of Peter Marshall's book, *Mr. Jones, Meet the Mas-*

ter. He was the Chaplain of the United States Senate. The book opened a window to allow a new breeze to enter into our fellowship. Marshall suggested that not only did Christ do the inviting, he invites people to come and leave behind all they have and all they will be. Or as Bonhoffer would say, He demands not just your confession, but your life. He came to the disciples and said, "Come." They arose and left what they were doing and followed him. Talk about costly! The price seems unreasonable and impossible. As I began to understand what Bonhoeffer meant and what Marshall was talking about, I became very disturbed. My inner-turmoil began to increase everyday. I prayed, studied and tried to resolve my conflict. Had I really made a commitment to Jesus Christ so deep and so pervasive that I could walk away from all that I have in order to follow where He would want me to witness? It soon became clear to me that my commitment was not that deep and complete. I had to face a question about the integrity of my witness. Evidently it was hollow. I was preaching and calling people to discipleship and refusing to make the commitment myself.

The next four years were years of turmoil and inner confusion. My congregation continued to grow. Our finances were solid. New people were coming in a steady stream to join our fellowship. The witness of the church was vital. We made commitments to stewardship as God's way of financing His community. Various other community and civic groups undertook moneymaking projects for outreach. Never did we have a money-making project for the church. We lived by what people were prompted to give. We had more than enough. My salary was increased every year. We had money to meet every program we implemented. It was during this period that Costly Grace, Called by Christ, and being formed into the image of Christ became powerful images in my own life and ministry. How would they play out in the life of a congregation? How would they take shape in my own life?

These years coincided with the McCarthy era in the USA. It was a time of great social unrest. Clergy and those in academia had their integrity challenged. Every profession seemed to be under attack. When I arrived in Cincinnati in 1956, I joined the local branch of the Fellowship of Reconciliation. Before long I was elected chair of the Cincinnati group. I never foresaw the personal attacks that would emerge. Several self-appointed vigilantes followed me wherever I spoke. They stood up at the end of the meeting to inform the audience that I was a Communist sympathizer and they were there to warn the people in the congregation that what I had been preaching was nothing but Communist propaganda. This went on continually. It began after I preached a series of sermons at a youth retreat on "Race-The Challenge to our Faith." I called the young people to begin to think for themselves. They need not be locked into the rigid categories that seemed to control the lives of adults. The future of America and the world was in their hands. Their witness would lead us to a new age and a new vision of the world. When the retreat ended, I drove straight home. Just as I pulled into my driveway, a pastor and a member of his church whose daughter had attended the youth retreat were waiting in the drive. She wanted to talk with me. Actually, she came to enlighten me about race and those who sought to break the barriers that separate people from each other. She informed me that my point of view was based on Communist ideology. Those whom I quoted, i.e. A.J. Muste, along with others were known Communists, she said. After an hour, they left. She spent the next several years informing the audiences wherever I spoke that they should beware of my Communist leanings.

My church was in an affluent area of Cincinnati, the Sycamore School District. Many of my lay persons did not share my views on war, peace, or race but my congregation never once came to me and said, "keep it cool". They would occasionally engage me in a conversation about the fact that we had such different viewpoints on some of the major issues of the day. Never did they demand I change my witness in order to remain as their pastor. I respected their right to have their views and they accorded me the privilege of arriving at my own conclusions. It was this mutual respect that enabled the church to grow even with the continual attacks against me from many sources. Their support gave me courage and a strength that I never knew before. Their affirmation has traveled with me to keep me on the path and my eye upon the Cross. It was Loyal and Billy Curfman, Ted and Etha Haas, Bill and Janet Lemon, Burt Davis and his family, Fred Leverenz family, Larry and Lou Acomb, Bob and Dorothy Miller, Mattie Dougman Stanley Atkins family, Laura Schwartz, Bill and Millie Black, Carolyn and Dick Pratt, the Fenstermacher's, Stanley's, Chuck Bautenheimer's, Toddy Hill, Forry's, Dulle's, Alene Branch, Dean and Faye Leonard, Hutchison's, Carl and Marianne Radtke and a host of other lay persons whose pilgrimage enriched life during these days in Montgomery. There would be many others whose names could be added to the list of dedicated lay persons who enhanced this journey.

It was the congregation who affirmed the church must be a model of what it preaches. It cannot just talk about truth and love. It must be truth and love. It cannot just talk about sacrifice, but must sacrifice to keep its integrity. Consequently, we set for ourselves goals that challenged our efforts. We strove for a budget of 50% for ourselves and 50% for others. We reached 48% by the time I left for Asia. We could not talk first about morality and ethics, unless we were willing to model what an ethical and moral church would be in this community and in the world. Bonhoffer explicitly affirmed the fact that the church is the Body of Christ. If it is the Body of Christ, it must have the form of Christ in every dimension. When people see the church, they should see Jesus Christ formed in human community. What a lesson Church of the Saviour(Methodist) taught me during those years. If we kept our integrity, we would draw all people unto Him.

Work Campers clearing land for the YWCA in Ceylon

Learning from a SE Asian Missionary Doctor

While I was searching to discover the direction for my life, I was constantly reading and trying to reason out what it was that God wanted me to do with my life. I seemed to be going in circles. I discovered a book written by Tom Dooley, a missionary doctor in Southeast Asia. As I read of his life and work, a light began to glow within me. I sensed the presence of God in a way I had not encountered Him before. I had not been praying or meditating. I was reading and suddenly it became clear, this was the direction I had to go in my life. While I felt deeply that I was to go somewhere in Asia to witness in love.

The Search Leads to Ceylon and India

By 1961, my search to understand the nature of the Call to Discipleship led me to apply to join the staff of the assembly of the World Council of Churches to be held in New Delhi, India in November and December, 1961. I was accepted. Plans were made to staff the Church of The Saviour during my three-month absence. I was to participate in a special work camp in Ceylon for three weeks. Then I would journey to New Delhi by way of South India to visit a classmate from Boston who was chaplain at the American College in Madura. Also, I would also spend a week at the Ashram of Vinoba Bahve, successor to Gandhi.

In Ceylon (today it is known as Sri Lanka), I would begin to understand what it means to give one's will so completely to Jesus Christ. I was one of two Americans in a group of 13 from around the world who were invited to share in this special work camp. Sri Lanka had been previously chosen to be the site of the 3rd Assembly of WCC. However, when a Buddhist priest killed the Prime Minister, Mr. Bandaranike, cultural conflict became a major issue in the country. The future of religious groups in Sri Lanka was so uncertain that it was necessary to move the assembly to New Delhi. The leaders of the World Council of Churches did not want to ignore what had been happening in Sri Lanka so they developed a work camp to witness in the midst of all that was happening in that land.

I was the last one to arrive at the work camp location, so there were no beds left. I could hear them attempting to move things around in the men's bedroom when I walked in the front door. I could hear them saying "What are we going to do? Who will move out and let the American have a bed?" By some mysterious force, I quickly stated I wanted to sleep on the floor. If they had a sleeping bag, I would be comfortable. They brought out a sleeping bag and room was made for it on the floor next to the bed of a young man from Kenya. After several days, I realized that scorpions lived in Sri Lanka. Previously, I had only seen them in books. It began to dawn on me the second or third day; that scorpions walk around on the ground, and perhaps on floors. After another night, I thought perhaps they would seek out a shoe to lodge in for the night. So each morning I would gently shake my shoes when I awoke. I was not disappointed. Two mornings later, the first of a number of scorpions fell out of my shoe as I turned it over and shook it each morning. About the sixth day, I began wondering about the sleeping bag. I had seen movies where snakes got in the sleeping bag. Would scorpions? I had no idea and really didn't want to ask. I prayed, "Lord I really didn't ask to be here. You brought me here for some reason. I don't know what you had in mind. But Lord, I am truly in your hands. I place my life and all I am at your direction. You can see I am confused and afraid. I need some steadying of my own understanding of Your will. Please God take my life and may you find it useful in your mission. Amen" I never worried about scorpions again. In fact, whatever occurred in the next two weeks, I celebrated the experience.

The next three weeks were a growing experience in eating spiritual food I had never encountered. I would do many new things from digging a foundation for a new YWCA, jumping into tropical lakes to bathe, Bible study, Compline, (Anglican word for evening devotions) all enlarging my understanding of life.

There were so many experiences in Ceylon that it is difficult to write about just one or two instances. However, I can summarize the experience by saying it opened my eyes and mind to a world I did not realize existed. In a multi-cultural setting one's perceptions and understanding began to shift. From Indonesia, Chile, Mexico, India, Ceylon, Borneo and other places, the cultural perspectives of the strangers I was learning to know, began to become part of my growing experience of God's diversity. I became aware of the vast variety of experiences which people share on the journey of responding to the call of Christ.

When I left, Ceylon I took a ferry to the most southern tip of India. I was the only westerner on the boat. Dawn had just broken and the boat slowly moved out of Colombo toward the unknown. My first shock was when I went into the small snack shop. I had learned not to expect anything familiar. Imagine my joy when I saw I could have a fried egg and toast for breakfast. No one spoke English, or if they could, they were not making themselves known to me. I took a deep breath and picked up a plate and helped myself to what I wanted to eat. I did understand how much I needed to pay at the cashier. After several hours, our boat arrived in India. As I left the gangplank and made my way to the customs station, I felt very conspicuous. No one allowed me to get in line. Everybody moved in front of me. I was turning around in the spot where I was standing, with my head whirling. I moved over to a customs official and asked where to go and he very gruffly motioned to a line. I got in line and waited. When I arrived at the customs official, I had to open up my suitcase to expose everything in it. After about 15 minutes of turning everything upside down, the inspector motioned me to repack my suitcase and move on to the Third Class area of the train.

I got on and sat down. Everyone on the train was uncomfortable the minute I stepped on it. A few minutes passed and five Buddhist priests got on our car. They motioned and directed one of their number to sit next to me. It was as if they were making fun of the priest. He turned his back to me and rode that way all the way to Madura, about a 45-minute ride. They kept jibing at him the entire trip. I suspected that he was a westerner who had joined the priesthood. His hair appeared blond even though it was very, very short. I never felt so much on exhibition in my life than on this short train ride. Each time I looked to the left or the right, up or down, it seemed that the whole car was staring at me.

This is the operating room in the Brigg's clinic. The bucket is the center where the doctor operates.

The next several days were fascinating. The first day I was at my friend's home, he scheduled us to visit a Leper Clinic run by Dr. Riggs, an American missionary. It would take us an hour or so by jeep to get to the clinic. We arrived there early in the morning. They had just begun setting up their tables and other equipment for the day. The doctor took a three-legged stool down to the side of the river, put it down and then he dug a hole in the ground about one foot wide and perhaps a foot deep. This would be his operating room for the day. He would do 35 surgeries on lepers with no anesthesia. At least 200 people had come to have their bottles filled with medicine for the immediate future. I was moved by the gentleness of the doctor and the patience of the nurses. Every person who came received personal attention; whether he needed 10 minutes or 30 minutes, it was given without question. Finally, as the sun began to set, the clinic closed and Dr. Riggs went back to his 120-bed hospital to do his evening rounds. He told me that he conducted five clinics like this every week. I was exhausted and found it difficult to imagine how he could have enough energy to complete his hospital rounds before bed. He looked forward to it with an eagerness that suggested that he had a deep source of strength from which he drew his energy and optimism. He would remain a constant inspiration to me through the years when I felt as if I wanted to just quit for a while and rest.

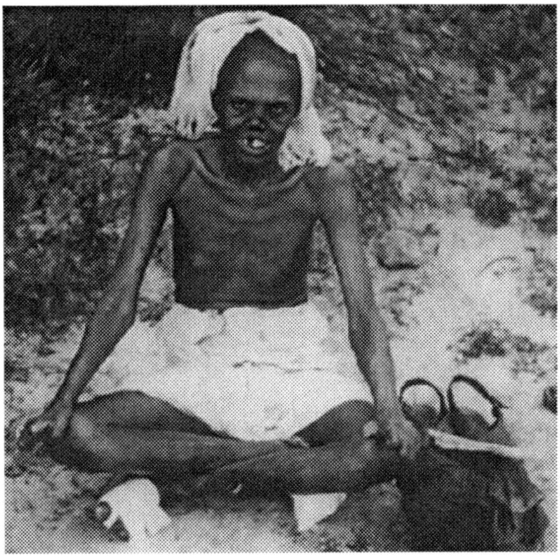

A Leper who was operated on during the clinic.

The next day I met a man by the name of Dick Keitan who took me to Ghandigram. This was the ashram founded by Gandhi. Vinoba Bahve had succeeded Gandhi as the head of the ashram. The Ashram was a center of prayer and reflection on life. They owned a number of acres of agricultural land. Many untouchables had come to live off the land. They pitched their small tents in the common ground in front of the main building. They tilled the fields and then shared in the produce. They gave me a tour of the land and of various projects they were operating in the villages, i.e. sewage systems. It would be a place where Gandhi and Vinoba Bahve and others would retreat for spiritual renewal.

Bahve was not there but his assistant Jakenadan led in prayer at 4 a.m. and oversaw a breakfast of peanuts and yogurt. The prayer services were in Hindi and the rituals were Hindu. Everything began to open new windows of understanding life and God's calling in the world. Encountering a German doctor who had lived for a year in the Ashram as he sought to understand his own personal destiny in life challenged my own journey. The memories of the Untouchables who lived outside our door and scratched out their meager existence are unforgettable.

Church in Madura where the author preached. Author is at left, pastor of the church, friend and missionary in India Bill Kelly.

On Sunday I preached in English at a Church of South India congregation in the heart of Madura. This would be my first sermon interpreted to another language. It was an amazing congregation. There was not enough room in the church so the congregation spilled over into the courtyard in front. It was a most responsive congregation and a rare worship experience for me.

The next morning, I boarded a plane to fly to New Delhi. As I took my seat, I noticed there was no one else on the plane but me. Just as I sat down, an Indian gentleman boarded. He wore the garb of an untouchable. He noticed that I was the only other passenger and took a seat directly across the aisle. He introduced himself as a member of Parliament and on his way to a session in New Delhi. I introduced myself, indicating that I was a Christian minister and was to participate in the Third Assembly of the World Council of Churches in New Delhi for the next three weeks. He commented that it sounded most interesting. He said," You must be the minister who preached yesterday in my district." It turned out that I had been in his home district. Then he began to tell me the story of his life.

He had grown up in Christian schools in his hometown. He had attended a Christian university and received his law degree from that institution. He commented that he often entered contests where the Bible was the principle source of questions. He said that he won more than he lost. In sharing his experience of being a lawyer in Madura, he commented that because of his Christian background and the wonderful education he had received, he was deeply concerned about the poor and the disaffected. He seemed to be so busy with clients who were poor that he had little time for much else. At that time in India, there was drive a by labor unions to organize labor in the factories. The government opposed the formation of unions. Many of the labor leaders were arrested and imprisoned. He was one of the few lawyers who expressed some social concern, so the labor movement appealed to him for help. He began to defend many of the leaders who were arrested for demonstrating and trying to organize various groups. After several years, the police came to his house and arrested him. He was charged with being a Communist and was found guilty and sentenced to prison. He commented that he was not a Communist and had not been aware that many of the people he had been defending were Communists. He spent the next seven years in prison.

Because his clients were mostly the poor, he had little money to adequately support his family. He began to worry about his wife and their three children. How will they eat? How will they buy clothes and medicine, etc.? After a week or so his wife came to visit him. She said "You will never guess what happened?" He anxiously answered "What?" "Yesterday a group of persons came with food and clothes for the children. They brought enough food that we will able to eat and care for ourselves for the next month." "Who were they?" he asked. "Were they from the church?" She replied," No, they were not from the church. They were from the Communist Party." He commented that for the next three years they never missed supplying food to his family and helping to meet their other needs. Not once during those years, people from his church never ever visited him or called on his family. After three years, he said, there was something about these people that was commendable. He wanted to understand them. So he asked to be given some literature and material that he could study about Communism. Actually, they continued to help his family the entire seven years. When he got out, he became a member of the Communist Party. He then said, "Today I am a Communist member of Parliament. I was to be part of an Indian delegation coming to your country to visit, but your government said that I would not be welcome as part of the delegation. Why is that?" I couldn't answer expect explain some of the hysteria associated with Communism during the past few years in the USA. He invited me to come to dinner at his house in Delhi. I politely declined his invitation. I was afraid that I would be in trouble when I got back home by having gone to his home. It would be guilt by association. How tragic it is that fear keeps us from enriching experiences which could only make one's life more meaningful.

When I arrived in New Delhi for the three weeks of the Assembly, I was stimulated by my experience on the plane. I was assigned to operate the switches that activated the microphones of the various delegates as the interpreters translated the conversations into many languages. For three weeks, I listened in on discussions of "how to evangelize in a Communist country", "how to witness in the midst of affluence," "how to witness in the face of persecution." I conversed with interpreters from Russia, Hungary, Germany, France and Spain. The debates on the floor of the Assembly, as the reports came from the various working committees, enabled me to listen in as the Christian World debated how they could witness in the midst of a revolutionary world. The theological discussions challenged all the old concepts that I had brought with me and they focused on the "Christic Presence" and the effort of the Assembly to understand what that meant for our age.

On my journey home, I stopped in Hong Kong. to visit Tao Feng Shan in a town called Shatin in the New Territories. Tao Feng Shan was a learning center for Buddhist priests and nuns who had become Christians. It was located at the top of a mountain. Here they studied to understand their new faith. I spent a day at the Center. It provided employment so the ex-priests and nuns could support themselves by their art. I also visited refugee housing units in various parts of Hong Kong. I talked occasionally with the people about their life and times in this new environment. The crowded conditions overwhelmed me. I was surprised to learn how much they had given up to flee their homeland and take up living in these new, cramped quarters. The smiles on their faces sent a message to me unspoken, but poignant. In unbelievable circumstances, people could find hope and promise for tomorrow. I found myself dedicating myself anew to a concern for these persons who were seeking so much from a world that seemed unaware of their pleas.

When I returned to the United States in December, 1961, I was in inner turmoil. For the next several months, I felt a deep pull toward Asia. I heard deep in my inner heart a call to "Come and follow." I would answer each call saying, I have responded. I would hear a reply, "No you haven't." "Grace is costly." "It costs you your life." "It is only when we lose it, that we can find it." I knew the truth of these words and had often preached on them. Now they were challenging me to put my life where my words had suggested others should stand.

In May, 1962, I was invited to lead devotions at a youth retreat of the Marimont Community Church in Cincinnati. On the second day, I focused on the rich, young man who went home rather than follow Jesus. I forcefully made my point about the commitment to give up what one has in order to follow. After devotions, I found myself on a bench watching a hot volleyball game. A young girl in her mid-teens sat next to me. After a few minutes she asked, "Have you ever?." I replied "Ever what?" "Have you ever given up everything that you had in order to follow Christ," she replied. My words had come back to haunt me. She had called me on what I had proposed to the young people. Did I have a right to ask others to make a commitment that I was not willing to make? I had to face the fact that my integrity was at stake. I had asked others to do what I was unwilling to do.

In June 1962, driving to Annual Conference, I shared with my wife the deep calling to offer myself to the Board of Missions. My preference would be Asia, mostly because I believed it was crucial in the years ahead. These churches needed to develop leadership for the gigantic burst of population that was emerging in almost every Asian country. We decided to send in our applications.

When we submitted our applications, I had a doubt that the Board of Missions was unaware. In the Army, I had had histoplasmosis. I was fairly certain that I would be rejected because of my lungs. I had not been able to secure any life insurance because of my health. I had a 30% disability from my military service in WW II. Everything was sent in, including the x-rays, etc. Now we would wait on the decision of the Board. While we were waiting, we had a telephone call from the Hollister's, retired missionary friends in Cincinnati. Mary told us that Dr. Harold Brewster, the Board doctor was in town and would enjoy meeting us to get acquainted. I suspected he had come to give me the word—we couldn't go. When we arrived, there were the normal greetings and introductions. After a while, I asked whether ill health kept people from missionary service. The Doctor explained that actually health was a factor they could use to filter out persons who would not fit into the missionary life. In my case, he thought health would not be a problem. We really might be accepted. "What have we started?", I said to myself. Before the evening was over, I had a calm feeling in my heart. Our conversations that evening filled us with anticipation for the future. Within weeks, we received word that we had been accepted.

We were off to Drew University for our first orientation as new missionaries. It would be a six-week study of South East Asia and linguistics. It was here that we were told that we would go to Yale to study Chinese after our orientation period. Following Drew, we would go to the Missionary Orientation Center in Stony Point, NY for three and a half months.

Our living unit family with whom we would be living during our time at Stony Point.

Just after we arrived at Stony Point, the publicity about the upcoming March on Washington was in all the newspapers. One evening several of us were talking in front of one of the fireplaces in the main building. The conversation got around to the March, maybe we should consider participating in it. As the discussion continued, it became clear that several of us felt deeply that our integrity demanded that we participate in this witness for civil rights. Finally, some of our group decided they would participate if we could arrange transportation. My wife was reluctant to go. She suggested there might be disorder and possible riots. We discussed this. Who would watch our children while we were gone? What if there were shooting and some people did not return? Was it fair for both of us to go?

After we discussed these questions, my wife decided to go and we were on the list. We arranged for another couple who would not be going to watch our children.

The night before the march, we were bused to New York where we joined with the United Church of Christ people who were to attend the march. We would ride in their buses. We met at the Broadway Tabernacle for a worship service at 10 p.m. After the worship service we had a sandwich and some beverages. We boarded the bus at 11:30 p.m. to leave New York at mid-night. We arrived in Washington at daybreak. The bus in which we were riding went to a United Church of Christ church located in D.C. We were told the church was prepared for us and were serving breakfast. When we arrived at the church, a warm welcome was extended by the congregation as we entered. Many Blacks were on the sidewalks watching as the buses rolled down the streets. No one waved or smiled. At the church, there was a festive atmosphere in the air. After breakfast, we all gathered in the sanctuary for a service of prayer before we left for the Mall. Senator Hubert Humphrey arrived to lead our service of worship. He gave a meditation that was a stirring appeal; and a prayer that the day would be a witness to a great truth—the equality of all people. Following the service, we boarded the buses. After a short ride, we found ourselves near the Washington Monument lined up behind hundreds of other buses. The buses emptied. We didn't know what was happening, but someone gathered us together and said follow them. We walked across the Mall to a place on the distant street to take our place in the line of march. As we arrived on the street, we were shocked to see the military lined up on both sides of the street holding rifles with fixed bayonets. We felt very uneasy at first. As the crowds increased, a jubilant spirit began to pervade. The time arrived for the March to begin and all moved out, arm in arm, black, white, red, tan, yellow. As we marched we began to sing "We shall overcome." The rest of the day has been recorded in history—the moving speech by March Luther King, the visit of a delegation to the White House and their welcome by the President, John F. Kennedy. After the rally we boarded our buses to return to New York. As we left Washington, the streets were lined by black folk waving and cheering as the buses moved out slowly to their destinations throughout the land. Only later, I would realize we had just participated in one of the great historic moments in the struggle for freedom. Participants on the bus were elated, energized and exhausted by the events of the day. We would never forget our involvement on August 27 1963; it was Charlotte's and my 14th wedding anniversary.

Family picture when we first arrive in Singapore in November, 1964.

ARRIVAL IN THE JUNGLE OF BORNEO

4

The Adventure Begins

"THE SIGN OF GOD'S PRESENCE WITH YOU IS THAT YOUR FEET ARE WHERE YOU DID NOT EXPECT THEM TO BE."

—*Red Bird Mission Banner, Kentucky*

In November, 1964, we arrived in Sarawak, East Malaysia, as Methodist missionaries. One of my early responsibilities was to supervise a small, rural, Chinese elementary and junior high school, located in the heart of an area that was plagued with anti-government activity. The community was called Tulai. The government would not permit any local person to be in charge of the school because they questioned the political loyalty of rural residents. If the school was to stay open, a missionary had to act as supervisor. That job fell to me.

Tulai Elementary School Facilities

Borneo Jungle Revelation

I will never forget my first trip to Tulai by speedboat from Sibu. It took about forty-five minutes until we docked at the outer jetty. It was a small landing about six foot square and made of slats of unfinished wood. It was slippery with moss from the humidity. A 6 foot section went from the jetty to the land. It had to be traveled cautiously, or you might slip into the river. This time I had brought my bicycle to ride the two miles through the jungle. The path was built up through the jungle swamp. It was about a foot wide and quite straight for that part of the world. I got on my bicycle and had gone about one mile when I noticed something in the path. I stopped about twenty feet from the object. It was a snake stretched out in the sun on the center of the path. It was iridescent green. It actually glowed as if plugged into an electric socket. What should I do? It looks like a snake that I have heard described as "a twelve step snake"-you go twelve steps and you are dead. I was terrified. I hate snakes. On the left side there was about six inches that I could go with the bike. I could pedal as fast as I could, put my feet on the handlebars to get by. At that point I said to myself, "What do I do if the snake gets caught in the wheels of the bicycle?" "Jump off and run", I reasoned. Off I went as fast as I could pedal. The snake never moved. I picked up the pace and rode my bicycle to the school.

On another occasion we were going to Tulai by speedboat. The tide was in, so we were able to take the small stream that went another mile toward the school. As we moved further inland, the stream narrowed. The weeds on the sides brushed our boat. The driver idled the motor, and we moved forward very slowly. He motioned to me to get up in front of him and stand on the front of the boat. He shouted, "Watch out for stumps!". We slowly turned to the right at a bend in the stream and there in the sun on the bank lay a huge krite, a black and white snake about eight feet long. I had never seen anything like it in my life. I motioned to the driver to look. His mouth went open. He was as terrified as I was. I stood motionless and softly said, "What do we do?" The driver said, "If he moves and tries to get in the boat, jump out the other side and run." "Run where?," I answered. He slowed the engine and we drifted slowly forward. Our eyes were glued on the snake. Slowly, we passed and it never moved. When we were safely away, Suliman turned up the engine and headed toward the dock at the inner jetty. Nothing in my life frightened me as much as the encounter in Borneo with snakes.

Fear had threatened to grab me, but the deep sense of purpose in my gut overrode any fear that wanted to emerge. This sense of what was right and appropriate has been the guide for my life. It is the source from which I know what is true. What is true is the presence of the Creator. When I reside in Him, every moment of the day, I have a deep sense of being where I should be at that moment. If I feel uncomfortable about what I am doing, I choose to wait until that assurance comes.

I believe God speaks to us if we are willing to wait and listen. It is in stillness that we hear what He has to say to us. It comes as intuition or a sense of increasing Light. In any case, that Light comes if one is receptive.

The experience at Tulai confirmed my conviction that those values that bring peace are at the heart of Christianity as in other faiths. I can share only those which I have discovered on my journey. I am indebted to Mahatma Gandhi for his insights and understanding of life and to Pundit Nehru from India for his witness and wisdom. I also owe much to Tolstoy and others.

My testimony is from an encounter with the gospel of Jesus—Jesus' own message—there is a way of being that moves beyond both the secular and the religious conventional wisdom.

"The path of transformation which Jesus taught leads from a life of requirements and measuring up (whether to culture or to God) to a life of a relationship with God. It leads from a life of anxiety to a life of peace and trust. It leads from the bondage of self-preoccupation to the freedom of self-forgetfulness. It leads from life centered in culture to a life centered in God."[1] This insight was to become a powerful force in my life through the years.

---

1. Borg, M.J., *Meeting Jesus for the First Time,* p.88.

5

It is in Relationships That We Exist

Without others, I am no one. Without a tribe a person has no name. It is in relationships that I exist and have my being. At the same time this other person is also a unique individual.[1]

During our first term in Sarawak, there would be many lessons we would learn. It was in Tulai that I learned a crucial lesson in my life—the importance of relationships.

The community of Tulai was about thirty miles from Sibu or 1 1/2 hours by speedboat. Because of open, community hostility toward the government, the state education office required a non-Chinese must be in charge of the school. I was appointed to take the place of a missionary who had supervised the school.

Tulai School Board L-R Mr. Lee, Author, Assistant Principal, Mr. Lau Chairperson, other three members.

1. This is from some of the writings of the author.

No one on the School Board could speak English, so Board meetings were held in Chinese, sometimes Foochow and sometimes Mandarin. I was apprehensive because I felt insecure with my command of Mandarin Chinese. I made arrangements for a Chinese pastor to accompany me and be my interpreter. School Board meetings were held once a week. Teng Yu Chi would go with me whenever we had a board meeting. It would take at least a full day to go and return to Sibu. After dark, it was too dangerous to be on the river because you could not see the floating logs and other debris, so we had to be back before sundown at 6:30 PM.

After several weeks of travel with the interpreter, I was having a problem of communicating with and understanding the Board. Some of the problems were related to the mistrust of the Chinese by the government. I sensed that we appeared to have a dead lock on the Board. Our chairman had been chosen because he was the only one who could sign his name.

Mr. Li, the principal, and I had talked about making improvements that we felt were crucial at the school. Teachers' morale was not good. The principal and I began to set aside the kick-back money we got from all our purchase of supplies, materials and books. There was always a 10% cash refund to the person who did the purchasing. A refund was given by each merchant to the individual who did the purchasing. In six months we had saved $10,000 Malaysian ringgit. We used the money to buy a generator for the school, new kitchen facilities for each teacher, new linoleum in their apartments, and new tables for the dining area. As the improvements were finished, there was an amazing transformation. The teachers became more contented. The School Board was pleased at the improvements. Yet, a tension existed between the Board and me.

Whenever I went to Tulai, I had to travel the final two miles in the jungle from the jetty where we docked our speedboat. The driver would stay with the boat, while I rode my bicycle down the narrow footpath through the rubber gardens to the school. The path was about eight to ten inches wide and on each side was swamp. On the second trip to Tulai, large red Chinese posters were nailed to the trees along the path. I could not understand them, so I pulled them down to take back to the theological school for my Chinese co-worker to translate. One poster read: "Red-headed devil go home." The next time I returned, there was another poster. It translated "We are like ghosts. We come and go in the jungle. Mao Tze Tung is our leader." I had at least four posters to greet me. The previous supervisor had reported this type of activity to the police. I decided not to mention it to any official. I had not come here to sow enmity but to help establish peace. Should I notify the police? I believed deeply that God had not brought me here to work with the police but with people and in the spirit of love and non-violence. The posters stopped after the fourth poster.

Communication at the school did not improve. I began to wonder if my problems might be in understanding the Chinese way of conducting meetings. Interpreting an American missionary's ideas into Chinese is not simple. Sometimes my interpreter would use Mandarin and other times he would switch to Foochow(a dialect of Chinese) that I did not understand.

A week after one of my trips to Tulai, I was invited to preach at a meeting of the Methodist Women of Sarawak. It was a large meeting and I was to preach on an assigned topic. I asked a pastor to interpret for me. By this time my understanding of Chinese had improved so that I could understand a sermon if I knew the context of the sermon. I began my sermon. I spoke in English and he interpreted me into Mandarin. Almost from the beginning, I sensed it was not easy to interpret what I was saying. So I spoke more slowly and listened more carefully. I noticed that he was not translating exactly what I said. He was using his interpretation of what I was preaching to translate. (According to Chinese custom it would not be appropriate to say that he misinterpreted one word in my sermon. He would lose face.) I made the decision that the time had come for me to be on my own. I must do my own speaking. I told the pastor that I really needed to make myself speak Chinese, so I wanted to try on my own from now on and if I had a problem, I would ask for his help. I would go to Tulai without an interpreter.

The next school board meeting we used Mandarin. Everything went very well. The Board struggled because they did not usually speak in Mandarin. After three weeks, we still had problems understanding one another. I knew that the Chinese could be very stubborn. I had often seen this at various meetings in the past. At our next meeting I was exasperated. I hit the table with my fist so hard the cups actually came up off the table and fell over. I said, "I am leaving." I walked out the door. The chairman, Mr. Lau, came running out to stop me. He caught hold of my arm and stopped me. He implored me to return. He assured me that they would listen and be helpful. We argued on the porch for about five minutes. I finally agreed to come back. From that time on our relationship was as solid as any relationship I have ever had with a group of people. We struggled together to develop plans for a new secondary school building. We would install the first running water in the community in the new chemistry laboratory.

The experience taught me that proficiency in the language is essential if you wish to work in any foreign environment. Only you can say exactly what you mean to communicate. It is impossible to be a responsible individual in any endeavor if you cannot communicate. I am amazed how many people depend on interpreters to conduct their business. Without an understanding of the language one is at a tremendous disadvantage in doing business. This could be said about working in any foreign environment.

I learned more about doing business with the Chinese during my experience in Tulai, than I could ever have learned in a classroom. When we had our secondary school building ready to break ground, there was a serious problem. There was no road to the community. How could we get the construction supplies to the school from the dock two miles away? We decided to hire anyone in the community who wanted to help to carry items from the dock to the building site. We would pay them according to a set fee that the principal had worked out.

Tulai Middle School. New building which we built to provide modern classrooms

As the school neared completion we needed to get new chairs and desks for the students. We needed to order gas jets for the science laboratory. Only one store in Sibu sold the lab equipment we needed for the school. The merchant wouldn't get the catalogue out for me to see. I went to the store every week for six months to drink tea and speak with the owner. Slowly, we became friends. Finally, he took the order book and took my order.

I needed to buy new desks and chairs. One of my students at the theological school had a brother in the furniture business. His store was next to my barber. Every time I went to the barber, I would stop to say hello. I went to him to buy the furniture we needed. It turned out I bought the furniture for less than any Chinese could purchase it. I had helped his brother on certain occasions. He was returning the favor with appreciation.

These two incidents illustrate a dimension of Chinese business that is often hard to grasp. They like to do business with people they know. Friendship is more important than the business transaction. However, business is important. If you have a good relationship with a Chinese businessman you do not have to worry about being cheated. You will get a fair price.

Relationships are central. As in everything, it takes time to establish a relationship. They are not based on my American view of life or business. When I venture into cross-cultural experiences, I have had to learn how to cross into another culture and communicate. Even in your own culture, relationships are basic to life.

I was fortunate to have had the opportunity to enter into Chinese life in a special way. I had to become secure enough to depend on my own ability to speak Chinese, if I hoped to give leadership in the Tulai School. I am certain that it is a barrier for a person to be dependent on others to explain what only you can explain yourself.

To have the confidence to build relationships with others is one of the important skills anyone can develop on their journey. Fame and fortune may come. Only relationships can sustain us. They are the givers of meaning to all our labor. It is from relationships that we receive the reward that comes from companionship and friendship.

L-R Rev. Yu Teck Soi, Rev. Wong, Rev. Ling Kie Hieng, Bishop Yap, Rev. Wong Lee Huo

When I first arrived in Sarawak, I was paired with Rev. Yu Teck Soi, the District Superintendent of Sibu. He spoke English and was invaluable to me during my early years in Sarawak; he became my mentor in understanding Chinese culture. As we went to meetings, he would share with me insights about how to establish a relationship with the Chinese, how to share ideas, how to earn their respect, etc. These insights proved to be the most valuable lessons during my time among the Chinese. He gave me the wisdom of his experience. I recall he recommended waiting at least four or five years before making a suggestion. This advice was the most important piece of information he shared with me. He suggested I spend the early years seeking to build relationships of trust and respect. Teck Soi would share Chinese idioms that would help his people perceive my immersion in their culture and life. These would be invaluable when I preached. On a number of occasions people chuckled when I used one of the sayings he shared with me. It was uncommon for Westerners to use such expressions.

One of the most vivid illustrations of the effectiveness of his advice to me was evidenced during the process of the church becoming autonomous. There was an older missionary who had been born in Foochow. He spoke fluent Foochow. He was one of the few missionaries who could speak that dialect. He had lived with the Chinese for many years. He appeared to have a good relationship with the pastors. When the local Chinese leadership constituted the committee to move toward autonomy, they invited me to be the missionary member. The older missionary was not invited. I was very uncomfortable with the selection, so I went to Teck Soi to ask what I should do in this situation. He said that it really wasn't open to my questions or fears. I should remain and make the contribution I could make at this time and place. He let me know that my appointment was not lightly made and the Chinese felt that I had more of a feeling for autonomy than the other missionaries in the Chinese Conference. I felt privileged but humbled by the appointment. This came after four years. In fact, it was really the first time I was selected to be on any committee in the Conference. Following this I would find myself on the committee that determined the distribution of funds from the United States. Also, I received an assignment to go with a local Chinese doctor to explain autonomy to people in a community up river from Sibu. Charlotte and I were fortunate to have cultural informants during our early years in Sarawak. These experiences and insights would guide us in our work in Sarawak as well as Singapore.

Dr. Ivy Chou, Principal of the Methodist Theological School, Sibu, Sarawak.

Occasionally the Dean of the Theological School, Dr. Ivy Chou would invite Charlotte and me to her home for tea or lunch. She would share with us some insight or understanding of Chinese culture to help us in our work with the students. Several months after our arrival, I was invited to speak at an MYF Retreat. The topic was "The blood of Christ." Ivy invited Charlotte and me for tea. Our conversation turned to the historical importance of blood in Chinese thinking. She knew that it was not a crucial aspect in my theology. I took her advice and had a great time with the youth at the retreat. Years later a local Chinese pastor, Wong Meng Tso came up and pointed a finger at me and said "Your sermon at the MYF retreat had a tremendous influence on my life. I have been trying to live out the meaning of a tent-making ministry ever since you preached that day." Little do we know how our words reach out to others.

The Chinese make relationships one of the core aspects of their lives. This is the reason that Yu Teck Soi and Dr. Ivy Chou spent so much time enabling us to understand the people among whom we lived and worked. This contribution would be a gift of invaluable proportions the rest of our lives. In fact, it is probably one of the most important experiences in understanding that I gained during my life.

After we returned to the United States I encountered a book by Dean Ornish which would emphasize the importance of relationships. He points out in his book LOVE AND SURVIVAL that "*relationships are about balancing and sharing power*".[2]

When one person feels attacked or judged, he or she does not feel empowered and perceives a power imbalance. One feels up and one feels down. Ornish asserts that "*sharing feelings rather than attacking or criticizing makes it easier for others to listen; listening leads to empathy, empathy leads to compassion, compassion increases intimacy; intimacy is healing*".[3]

Trust is an essential element in relationships. Without trust, there is no relationship worth speaking about in any person's life. When trust is lost, it is not easily restored. There is nothing more critical in cross-cultural experience than trust. There is probably no more difficult cross-cultural task than to develop, within and outside the family.

As I have traveled through the various stages of my life, one fact has become clear, relationships cannot be built on conflicting value systems. We can maintain an acquaintance with someone who holds different values; however, it is almost impossible to move to an intimate sharing and caring relationship with someone whose values are in conflict with your own. It is not just the result of one generation failing to communicate with another generation. Values are key ingredients in quality relationships with people. If the value conflict is not faced openly and honestly, relationships can only move from bad to worse.

When one is living within another culture and seeking to work with some effectiveness he becomes a great advocate for pluralism. There are many ways to do things. My way is only one of a number of ways in which something can be done. I have learned that my way is not the only right way to do something. In fact, my way could often inhibit something from occurring in the lives of others. The Chinese enabled me to understand that there are many ways to do something. The secret is to find the way that is appropriate for the place and time in which you find yourself. Relationships are the foundation of life; nurture and tend them with great care.

---

2. Ornish, Dean, LAS, p. 104.
3. Ornish, Dean, LAS, p. 124.

6

The Dance of Life

Golden breaks the dawn,
Comes the eastern sun,
Over lake and lawn
Set his course to run.
Birds above us fly,
Through the earth and sky
God's great mercies flow.[1]

In 1966 I was a delegate of the theological school at a seminar in Hong Kong on "Rapid Social Change." It was an experience which stimulated many new insights to challenge my teaching and living. One occurred on a Sunday afternoon. We were located at Chung Chi College in the New Territories. On our breaks, two delegates from Japan and I often talked together. Outside the building in which we were seated was a beautiful garden. One group of people after another stopped and took photographs of the beautiful garden and their loved ones. One of the Japanese friends commented: "This illustrates one of the differences between Japanese and Westerners." I didn't get what he meant and I asked for a further explanation. He said, "You take a picture of Nature, but when we go out into the garden, we allow God or Nature to look at us." The different way of looking at life became a new understanding for me in my relationships with students and co-workers. Later I would find this comment clarified by Suzuki.

Commenting on the Biblical view of man found in the story of the Fall described in the Garden of Eden story, Daisetz T. Suzuki observed that Man is against God, Nature is against God, and Man and Nature are against each other. God's own likeness (man), God's own creation (nature) and God himself—all three are at war. Commenting on the Oriental view, he said, "Nature is the

1. East Asia Christian Conference Hymnal, no.184, Chinese hymn, T.C. Chao (verse).

bosom whence we come and whither we go. Nature produces man out of itself; Man cannot be outside of Nature. I am in Nature and Nature is in me."[2]

Daisetz Suzuki forced me to look again at my faith with a new set of eyes. In the traditional Christian view, the eternal war is an assertion that is the basis of traditional Christian theology.

In more recent years, I have experienced new insights that suggest another interpretation of the condition of man that is plausible and possible. One who introduced me to the new interpretation is Matthew Fox, who has attempted to remove the veil that has so long been over our minds. In his development of the Creation Atonement, he has enabled Christendom to view a viable alternative to the Crucifixion Atonement based on the "eternal war" assumptions. The Creation Atonement asserts that God and man have never been separated. A loving God has kept a constant relationship with His creation.

In the Crucifixion Atonement, it is essential that someone or something restores the relationship with God that was lost with the introduction of human sin into the world. The sin has kept man and God separated from each other. Therefore, it has been necessary to have someone restore the lost relationship. It was the crucifixion of Jesus that restored the lost unity of God and man. His resurrection is an indication of the fact of restoration.

Fox's work, however, envisions a world in which God has never been separated from humankind or from His Creation. His view and Native American Spirituality are very similar. God created all that exists. God's Creative Process birthed life and He breathed His breath into it. He has been a part of all that is since it first became what it is today. He has not been separated from His creation, nor has He left life unattended.

There is a healthy wholeness in the view that Suzuki has suggested. We can learn from Asians a new way of understanding of life. In the Native American perspective, there is harmony and rhythm found within all of Creation. Native people have always seen themselves as part of the infinite rhythm and balance surrounding humankind. Christians, by tradition and choice however, have intentionally limited their vision. They have limited their perception and experience of life to the Bible. Certainly, the Bible is one of the more significant books in human history. I would never deny this fact. It has been for me a source of spiritual insight, guidance, and strength. Yet, my journey led me to work in Asia for seven years and introduced me to a wider world than I had ever imagined. It was

2. Suzuki, Daisetz T., "The Role of Zen in Buddhism" in Olga Fröbe Kapteyn, ed. *Eranos-Jahrbuch, 1953 (Zurich: Rhein-Verlag, 1954), p.294.*

a perspective that had insights about life that differed from my own. I have had to look at my own system of beliefs and ask how they accommodate my experience within other cultures. In fact, I have grown to understand that in the search for truth, other peoples and cultures have discovered and uncovered many profound insights into life and its meaning.

A cultural orientation infused only with the insights of Hebrew culture or European cultures represents a small part of the gigantic multicultural world which is the handiwork of the Creative Process. The testimony that is shared in the New Testament at Pentecost affirms the diversity at the heart of life. This diversity is not to be denied or destroyed, but to be celebrated. The significant aspect of Pentecost was that people each heard in his/her own tongue the Presence of the Spirit. No one translated for them.

This new understanding that is seeking to emerge in the midst of a confused and hate-filled world is a new comprehension of humankind's relationship to the Creator, to Nature, and to each other. It could be called becoming aware of "The Dance of Humankind". In many places, new insights bring us an understanding of the harmony and rhythm of life. The antagonisms that have dominated the national life of so many nations must end. We hear the cry of the Creator as the voice of one crying in the Wilderness, "Prepare the way for the people." "Open the doors of your minds", "Open your eyes to the beauty of a world filled with people of many races and many cultures." God's all-encompassing Being beckons us to join in the dance of humankind to the beat of the drums of many tribes.

An encounter between groups who are different from each other, i.e. African Americans and European Americans, Native Americans, Chinese Americans or people of Hispanic background is experienced with great anxiety. The anxiety comes because our contacts have been so infrequent and so superficial that we have had little opportunity to build relationships of trust and love. Those who are different from us, we hold at a distance, and at the same time, we have sought to reach out and touch them. Sometimes, I have wondered why we do that? I suspect that we do it because we are expected to do it. For the Christian, we do it because we heard that God expects this from each of us who are committed to Him through Jesus Christ. We do it out of duty and not love. In that sense, the reaching out is filled not with emotions and feelings of love and acceptance, but fear and suspicion. What we don't know or understand, we look upon with suspicion. We are reluctant to embrace it before we understand what it can and does mean for our lives.

Does Jesus teach an eternal enmity at the heart of humankind and Creation? Does *agape* love mean that we should be partially open to those who are different?

Does *agape* love suggest a vulnerability and openness toward others that compels one to reach out inspite of fear? Does love demand that we seek to move out in trust that humankind is bound together by a common humanity?

I believe love means acknowledging a common humanity enfolded within God's creative process. Love is renewed and strengthened as it joins in the harmony and rhythm of life. I believe love compels us to see each culture as a unique expression of the inner power of life. I believe love thrusts us into life with a sense of wonder at the diversity of hues and tongues that God has birthed. I believe those who love witnesses to the fact that Creation is one great symphony of life with the rhythm of the sea and the wind carrying the melody throughout the universe.

Matthew Fox has opened a window and the breeze has blown through it. The old smells and odors are gone. Fresh air now permeates life. This is the witness of all Creation. This is the witness of God revealed to us in all of His manifestations.

Jesus opened the windows and the doors of Judaism to the winds of diversity. People were not prepared for this new breeze. The old ways were the only way. They could not permit the new experience of diversity to grow. Because Jesus represented a threat to the commonly accepted way of living and doing things, he could not be tolerated. They crucified him. It didn't work. The Creator could not be stopped. What God creates cannot be killed. Jesus was buried in a tomb. He burst forth. Truth cannot be contained. Truth cannot be confined to a narrow and limited point in time or place. Truth is truth everywhere in Creation. Life is not within the power of man to give or to take. The Resurrection occurred. Some have disputed it. Many have sought to discredit it. Yet, as sure as the sun rises in the East, the spirit of God lives. Like it or not, Jesus lives. Nothing can and will ever stop the birthing of life and love. Wherever love is encountered, where forgiveness is exercised, where confession is acknowledged, there we find *agape*, and where *agape* is encountered we will find people face to face with Jesus Christ. *Agape* may not be dressed as a Jew or in any of the familiar trappings we associate with Jesus. It may not even be in the form of a man or a woman. It will be there. It cannot be ignored or denied. This presence pervades all of Creation for the all-encompassing Being whom we call God is LOVE. This is the Creative Process that surrounds and sustains life.

In 1963, we were at a missionary orientation learning linguistics. Bishop R.O. Hall, an Anglican Bishop who had been in China for forty years, shared with those of us who were going to Asia. He told us a story of a rural village of 800 in south China. It was a poor agricultural community. In fact, it was so poor that once every generation they held a community meeting. In this meeting they would choose a young person to be sent by the community to the city to receive an education. Only if the entire village shared its resources was it possible to get enough money to send one young person in each generation for an education. Each family knew that if their child was not chosen, he would remain like the parents, illiterate and uneducated. Bishop Hall then commented that this village exemplifies the self-sacrifice embodied in the heart of the Christian message and the witness of Jesus. In that community, he said Christ was present, whether consciously recognized or not. He said that we would find that wherever we go in the world, we would discover that Christ is present even though the Bible may not be in any home, since wherever the spirit of self-sacrifice is manifested, Jesus is present. Just imagine, if there was no missionary to proclaim it, but he is there. I have never forgotten the impact this story had on my life and work. It put in perspective my role in the Kingdom.

Missionaries often have an inflated idea of who they are and what they are about. It is in the humble acceptance of the wonderful opportunity to cross cultural boundaries that we find our most moving experiences. We came to learn and grow, not to direct and dominate. We came to free people, not to bind them and limit them to Western faiths. We came to share in an adventure in cross-cultural living that was unique. If our attitudes and life are open, we are invited to share in the life of a people who were and are very different from us. It is a privilege to experience another culture. The responsibility this brings to the individual is awesome. Bishop Hall enabled me to experience a birth of openness that has so enriched my life that I am forever indebted to him and to the Chinese people who allowed me to enter into their homes and lives.

On Palm Sunday, 1964, we were in New Haven at Yale University. We were in the midst of our study of Mandarin when we read in the paper that Paul Tillich would preach at Yale Chapel on Sunday. I had read everything Tillich had written to that point in my life. Now we could hear him preach in person. We arrived at the chapel thirty minutes early only to discover that it was almost full and seats were in the aisle. Tillich would preach on "self-sacrifice". He shared with us his insights on why Jesus was entering into Jerusalem. "He came," Tillich said, "as a man facing his own death. He knew what would happen if came into the city. He made a deliberate decision to confront those who would destroy him. He willingly came and gave his life." Tillich helped me understand the human dimensions of choice. To give one's life, willingly when you do not have to do it is an expression of a deep commitment. If it demands giving of one's life, so be it. Jesus didn't have to go to Jerusalem. He knew what would happen if he did. If he didn't, what would happen to his disciples and followers? Jesus knew that what he had taught his disciples and followers about love and life and it was up to him to illustrate it. He would give flesh and blood to the abstract ideas he had been preaching these several years. Now he would give them an example of the power of love in the face of evil. Tillich kept emphasizing that Jesus chose to enter Jerusalem. He chose to give his life. He chose self-sacrifice over self-preservation. In the end, he illustrated the truth that such a life witnessed to a love and truth that could never be stamped out. Tillich's words that day illustrated the truth Bishop Hall had shared with us in his story from China.

7

A New Understanding Emerges

In this time of sore distress,
Hidden danger round us press;
Life's true way we cannot find,
Fears and fancies fill the mind.
Saviour, give us eyes to see
Thy great Kingdom that shall be.[1]

The notched log was only six inches wide. Each notch barely accommodated the tips of our shoes. I cautiously walked up the log, while the welcoming faces at the top encouraged us on our climb. As I stepped onto the porch of the long-house, our hosts greeted us. Some women wore dirty bras over a blouse. Our group leader saw my face and softly commented to me. "They wear the bras because Western women wear then. They think it's the modern thing to do."

On the way back to town, the land rover bounced back and forth on the dirt road. A mile ahead, a car was off the road. It wasn't in a ditch, but just a wide spot, where it had come to rest. We stopped to see if there was any trouble. No one was around. We got out and felt the oppressive heat of the tropical sun as it relentlessly beat down upon us. We walked a few yards off the road into the jungle. Up ahead was a longhouse. Our conversation alerted the residents of the longhouse and two men came out to meet us. Each wore a white shirt with three pens in their shirt pocket. After a question about the car, we discovered that it had quit running at the spot where it stopped. Our informant told us that this was quite common. The people here did not realize that you had to put more gas in the car when it ran out. They had little perception of what propelled the vehicle. So they assumed it had just ended its usefulness. As we left, the informant also noted that the pens are interesting. Neither man could read nor write but in

1. EACC Hymnal, 1964, words by Y.L. Yang. no. 151.

town they had seen Westerners with pens in their pockets and assumed that this was the right thing to do when wearing a white shirt.

Iban young man on the front porch of his longhouse on the Rejang River.

Several months after our arrival an incident occurred between the police and a Punan. The Punan are a migrant tribe of natives in Sarawak. Some of them have longhouses and practice settled agriculture. Most of them have no specific location they call home, except the place where they are located at the present moment. They are primarily hunters and gatherers. They live far in the interior of Borneo. They eat wild sago and birds that they shoot with their blowpipes. They are very skillful with the blowpipes. They also hunt animals and gather fruits from the jungle. Most of them are not educated. In fact, they just do not have schools. Much of the life of the various groups in Sarawak is totally outside of the experience of the Punan.

One day, a Punan wandered into Kapit, located about 90 miles up river from Sibu where we lived. When the young man arrived in town, he wandered around looking at the shops and eating stalls that lined the street. At some point, a policeman saw him and went over to find out who he was and what he was doing in Kapit. At that time the government had a confrontation with Indonesia and everyone had to carry a pass in order to travel. The pass was an identity card with photograph. Of course, the Punan had no identity card. He probably did not even understand what it was the police wanted to see. He could not understand because he did not speak Malay that was the language spoken by the police. They took his confusion and inability to understand as an excuse to take him to the Police Station for further questioning. When they arrived at the police Station, he was taken into a small room and seated at a table. It was probably the first time he had ever sat in a chair and at a table. The building was a cement stucco structure that he saw for the first time. After they questioned him for a while, they were making little progress, and securing almost no information. The police seemed to be unaware that the Punan could not understand anything they were saying. They took a break from their questioning and left the Punan man in the room by himself. He was frightened. He noticed that there was a small window in the room He got up and looked out the window. He fiddled with it for a moment and discovered how to open it. It opened easily. He immediately crawled out and began to run toward the nearest cover of jungle that he could see. It was behind Christ Hospital, located on a hill about 100 yards from the Police Station. When the police discovered that he had crawled out the window, they began to blow their whistles and shout. They ran outside to see where he had gone. They saw him heading for the hospital area. As they gained on him, he desperately looked for a place to hide. He hid in a drain ditch. The police saw where he went and were on top of him within minutes. This time they handcuffed him and transported him to Sibu and to the government jail.

The papers were full of the flight of the Punan in Kapit. They indicated that he would have a trial in Sibu. Until the trial date he would be held in the prison. Just a day or so after he arrived at the Sibu prison, another unfortunate incident occurred. It was mid-morning and everyone in the prison was busy with their duties. Some of the prisoners, including the Punan could walk around the prison to go to the showers or rest room or speak with other prisoners. The prison office was not in a secure location. The main office resembled what we would call a picnic shelter. It had a roof and sides on the one side toward the street. The interior was completely open. People were at their desks busy with their work, including the Warden. The Punan wandered out of his cell and was going by the office. He saw a parong lying on a desk. A parong is a sword-like weapon and a sharp tool used by the natives to cut and slash the jungle. It is about three feet in length and very sharp. The Punan picked up the parong and he went directly to the desk where the warden was working and cut his head off. The government announced the next day that the Punan would be taken to Kuching, the state capital. He would be tried for murder. He was found guilty and sentenced to life in prison.

Everything about this experience is tragic. From the very beginning, the Punan was caught in a situation he did not understand, from the experience of life in Kapit, identity cards, strange language, and a city he had never seen, and a jail he could not understand, until he saw a familiar tool and an opportunity to slash his way out.

The Punan knew little about atomic bombs and nuclear energy. They may have never ridden in a car or truck. They have seen outboard motors on small boats. As they encounter the invasion of their home jungle areas by strangers who want the natural resources of gold, aluminum, and other precious metals, how do they respond?

The Punan cannot be free of outside influences. It is almost impossible to be isolated in our present century. The cultural changes which are coming will come as a stranger. It was birthed by other cultures and in other lands.

We need to remember that it took the Western world many centuries to accommodate to the industrial revolution and the upheaval it brought to every western nation. The Punan will need to adjust in ten or twenty years to that which took centuries in the West.

As I recall the tragic experience of the lone Punan, I cannot say that he was totally at fault. Justice would demand a life for a life. Do we not see another example of the inability of one culture to understand another. Whose actions were wrong? What made the law of Sarawak mandatory for the Punan? Can justice be so easily defined that situations like the Punan and his conflict with the police are listed as unfortunate, but necessary?

8

Surprising Sacrifices Are Required

Life is burdened down with care,
Dreams like bubbles burst in air;
Human hopes are empty things
Like dead trees and dried up springs;
Grant us, Prince of Life, we pray
Life abundant every day.

—Chinese Hymn, words by Y.L.Yang[1]

We make decisions but do not always realize the implications of them. During the time we were deciding whether to apply for missionary service, we talked openly with our children. We answered their questions. There were few. Little did I realize what sacrifices we would have to make in our family life. It was not long before the impact of our choices became quite clear.

Most children do not have a choice whether they will go with their mother and dad. It is just assumed they will go. We made this assumption. What we found was that we had brought our children with us for a new way of life. Instead of being the settled life that they were used to, life was constant adjustment. Not only did they adjust to new schools and new communities, but also strange languages, customs and cultures. Everywhere there were new sounds and smells.

The family life of a pastor in the United States is difficult. We move regularly to new assignments. Our eldest was Jill who was eight and was born just before we moved into our first parsonage in 1954. She would spend every Sunday morn-

1. East Asia Christian Conference Hymnal 1964, Kyoto, Japan, Editor D.T. Niles. no.151.

ing in the church nursery. Every Sunday evening, a couple from the church would pick her up and look after her while Charlotte and I led the youth programs. Tom was born at the end of our second year in 1956 in Willshire, OH, the first parish. At the end of the third year, we moved to Cincinnati to start a new congregation.

During the next six years, we lived in Montgomery, Ohio. I was busy calling on new people, and building committee meetings to plan the development of the new congregation. We finally decided that if I was to have any time at all with the children we would have to find some way to have supper together in a quiet place each evening. We discovered that one of the county parks would give us a wonderful place to play and eat for a couple of hours.

Thanks to the Quakers, mealtime was for us the celebration of the gift of life, a sacramental act in our family life. It was here that God is made real to all of us-in the breaking of the bread—we shared the Presence. This became an unspoken ritual in our family. Even today when we are together, it is not uncommon for us to spend 1 or 2 hours at the table talking and sharing or just catching up. Howard Thurman often made the comment during my days in theological school that "being together with an other" is one of the most important experiences in life.

During our time in Borneo and Singapore, mealtime was one of the daily experiences we kept at the heart of our family. There is one thing that has nagged me over the years. On so many occasions, ministerial responsibilities took me from our family time.(deaths, serious illness, accidents, family crises, church meetings, visitation of new families in the community and church, involvement with the PTA, district, and conference responsibilities) Family life was squeezed into the unfilled moments between responsibilities.

The decision to make ourselves available to the World Division of our Board of Missions of The Methodist Church was a joint decision that was made by Charlotte and me. Tom and Jill were very young and it was difficult to involve them directly in the decision.

After we were accepted, we had to arrange to pay our debts before we left. We could take no furniture to Asia, so we had to sell all household items. Among the furniture was a piano that we had bought for Jill. She was looking forward to learning to play it. But of course, the piano also had to be sold. We found a buyer for the piano and hoped he would come for the piano while Jill was still at school, but just as they were pushing it out the front door, Jill came running up the front sidewalk shouting, "My piano, they are taking my piano." Her mother tried to comfort her, explaining that it was too large to take to Asia.

That evening I was to speak to the Men's group at Armstrong Chapel Methodist Church which became one of our supporting churches. Of course, my talk changed after our afternoon crisis with the piano. My comments related to my daughter's reaction to the piano sale over which she had no choice.

We had to sell everything in order to pay our outstanding car debt to the Credit Union. After everything was sold, we fit two children, and our clothes in the car and had $400 in our pockets. In one sense I never felt as free as when our car pulled out on the long trip to New Jersey. We were to report to Drew University for South-East Asian area studies and linguistics for six weeks. Our children could not attend.

This became the first of many challenges in our missionary life. We had to find a summer camp for our children for six weeks. Fortunately, I had contacts in camping and contacted Leonard Ferguson from College Settlement Farm Camp in Hatboro, PA about a good camp near Madison, New Jersey. He recommended Camp Onas, a Quaker camp in the Delaware Water Gap region. We would entrust our six-year-old and eight-year-old to the care of this camp for the next six weeks. Tom and Jill didn't realize what was happening when we left them at the Camp. We were asked not to visit for three weeks. That was to be a long three weeks. Fortunately, Jill could write and did write several letters which helped us live through the experience. It was good preparation for what was to follow. The most difficult aspect of the summer was dropping the kids off at the camp. The schedule at Drew University was very intensive and the strain of having to send the kids to camp was just about the limit of the emotional resources that Charlotte and I possessed.

At the end of six weeks, we picked up our children and headed to the Missionary Orientation Center in Stony Point, New York. We would be there from August through December, 1963. We lived in two bedrooms, one for the children and one for the parents. We were housed in a community setting of five families. We shared shower and toilet facilities, living room and kitchenette. This would be our home for four and a half months.

Eight people were assigned to each table in the dining room. We shared a table with the Kim Young Soon family during our training. It became apparent from our first meal that we might have problems with our kids. They began to use the ploy that they didn't like this or that food. Charlotte and I talked about how we could handle this and not create an embarrassing situation. We told Jill and Tom that we expected them to take a little of all the food that is served. If they took it themselves, they could take a small spoonful. If they didn't, their mother or I would help them and give them at least 2 spoonfuls. After that we had no problems about food.

Jill and Tom were enrolled in the Stony Point Public School. Tom was in the second grade, and Jill was in the fourth.

During that period the parents had one set of activities and the children had another. We saw each other at meals and at bedtime. When school began, it was a struggle to find family time in the schedule. We had a few free hours on Saturday and again on Sunday afternoon. We found a few hours to visit Bear Mountain in New York.

In January, we arrived in New Haven, Connecticut, to begin Chinese language study at Yale University, Institute of Far Eastern Languages. Our classes were to begin on Monday at 8 a.m., but we could not move into our apartment for one month. We had to find some place to live for a month. We settled for the Hotel Adams, located in downtown New Haven, just south of the square. We rented a furnished suite for 30 days. What a shock! We moved in on Thursday. The black carpet and couch was sticky with an oily substance. We covered the couch and chairs with clean sheets so we could sit. On Sunday, we attended the closest Methodist Church. The church loaned us their sweeper and we spent the rest of the day cleaning. The stickiness remained.

Jill cleaning the room in the Adams Hotel, in New Haven.

The next problem was getting the kids to school. We had to be at our classes before their school started. The main post office in New Haven was across the square from our hotel. A public bus left there at 7:30 a.m. on a route directly to their school. Every morning, we dropped them off; they boarded the bus when it came and got off at the school stop and walked a block to the school.

In January, New Haven has an abundance of snow. Early in the term we awoke to an icy, snowy morning. We managed to get the kids to the bus stop and walked to our classes at Yale. After we arrived at class, Charlotte could not stop worrying. After the first class, she called the school to ask if the children were there. They had not arrived. The school promised to call the minute they arrived. Shortly, the phone rang and they told us that Jill and Tom had arrived safely. Their bus had broken down, but they finally made it. This was one of a number of stress events that happened over those six months.

Finally, our apartment near the school was ready for us and we moved in around February 1. A few days later the school sent word that Tom was having difficulty reading. Charlotte spoke with the teachers, and they arranged for Tom to work with a remedial reading teacher. He performed a miracle and got Tom caught up and motivated him to read up to his potential reading level. Again, because we had to be in class earlier than Jill and Tom, we had to leave them at home by themselves in the morning. We made arrangements with a neighbor to make sure they got to school each day. Talk about stress. Is it any wonder that by the end of February, Charlotte had a serious case of bronchitis and the Yale Health Service admitted her to the student hospital for several days. I am not sure how I coped, but apparently, we got through that week.

Yale Institute of Far Eastern Languages gave at least six tests a day in the Chinese program. If you did not get a 'B' on the test, you had to repeat it at night as a make-up examination. Every night, I had to repeat every test because I did not get the appropriate grade. Every evening after Jill and Tom went to bed, I would begin my homework that took at least two hours. It was obvious that an extra gift of grace would be needed if I was to successfully complete the Chinese program. With my language aptitude in the 12th percentile, it was obvious I had a challenge. The extra grace came and I did complete the course with a 'C'.

When summer arrived, another decision confronted us. Our language study would run through most of August. What would we do with the children? Tom and Jill went to the day camp at the YMCA in New Haven. Following the day camp, some of our friends from Ohio, Ralph and June Shunk and Mittie and Russ Sawmiller, volunteered to pick them up and take them to Martha's Vineyard until our session ended. At the end of Chinese study, we picked up the children and returned to New Haven to close our apartment and sell our car. On our last day in New Haven, we reached an agreement to sell our car. We were to return to Ohio for our Commissioning Service to be held at Armstrong Chapel in Cincinnati, Ohio, in late September, 1964.

Again, our friends took care of Jill and Tom because we were scheduled to meet with various groups at the church all weekend. An interesting event of the weekend was the effort by a pro-McCarthy group in the Cincinnati District and the sponsoring church proponents of the political right behind McCarthy to stop our commissioning service. Years latter, I learned about those efforts when the pastor told us about the events that occurred. At several of the events that weekend, I did notice that copies of *None Dare Call It Treason* were passed out to anyone who wanted a copy. This was one of the efforts in Cincinnati to blacken my name with charges of "Communist."

The Commissioning Service would involve only Charlotte and me. Since we wanted to include the children in the event, we arranged for Bibles to be presented to them during the service. Following the service, we were to leave within a week for San Francisco, where we were to board the *Kingsville*, a freighter for Singapore.

On our arrival in San Francisco, we discovered that our freighter was delayed and would not leave for a week. The local office of the Board of Global Ministries made arrangements for various persons to take us to the zoo and other places of interest in the area.

Tom, Jill and Charlotte on board the Kingsville at high sea.

It was late September and most schools were busy with the new term. We had enrolled Tom and Jill in the Calvert Correspondence course in Baltimore, for persons who needed help in places where education of children was a problem. We had planned to use Calvert for the first year. Charlotte held classes with the children each morning on the ship after we left San Francisco. It took three weeks for us to finally arrive in Singapore as our ship avoided sailing into a typhoon just north of Luzon in the Philippines.

After several days of orientation in Singapore, we flew to Sibu, Sarawak. We arrived in Sibu the first week in November. Joanne Sutlive, a missionary mother of two children the same ages of Jill and Tom proposed setting up a class room at her house to teach the Calvert course. There would be five children in the class, our two children, Joanne's two children and the daughter of the Philip's, a British Methodist missionary couple. It was a wonderful opportunity for our two children. They immediately had playmates and friends. While they were at school we, continued our Mandarin Chinese language study with a tutor, Mrs. Roger Peng from Hunan, China.

Jill and Joanne Sutlive in the new school room in Sibu.

Our early days in Sarawak were filled with adventure. We spent afternoons exploring the town and trying out our language skills in the market. As we biked around Sibu, we became increasingly familiar with the sights, sounds and smells in the *pazaar* (business district) downtown. We became very proficient with our bicycles, especially at riding and holding an umbrella in one hand to protect ourselves from the sun. Sibu is located at 1° north of the Equator It was very hot and humid. By noon it was usually close to 110°, and had over 250 inches of rain a year. It rained almost one hour every day. In the January rainy season, it usually rained for 20-30 days without stopping.

The adjustments for Jill and Tom were no easier than they were for us. We all had to find new friends and become familiar with our new environment.

Our first home was in a Malay compound. All our neighbors were Malay, an ethnic and linguistic group who had their own language and were Muslims. All the houses were about six or seven feet off the ground on stilts. This would protect us from high water during the rainy season. Under our house, we had a cage for chickens. The chickens were Tom and Jill's attempt at their first agriculture adventure. Behind our house was a private secondary school. The path to the school went directly under our house and through our yard. We were a ten-minute walk to the schoolroom where Jill and Tom had their classes or a five-minute bike ride.

Several months after we arrived, we moved to Hin Yu Park Road, nearer to the Methodist Theological School on Queensway Road, where both Charlotte and I had been invited to teach. By this time, life for the adults was finding a rhythm and a schedule. Jill and Tom were also developing a routine with school. In the Hin Yu Park neighborhood, Tom developed a friendship with two Chinese boys his age, Colin Tiong and Danny Teng, who spoke English. They quickly became friends and playmates.

At that time most of the other missionary children except the five children in the Sutlive school lived in the Mission Hostel in Singapore and attended the Singapore American School.

Within the first month of our arrival, we were invited to go with the Conference Methodist Youth Fellowship on a retreat to Mukah. We had no idea of Mukah's location or what the trip would entail. Our specific assignment was to be the advisors of the Conference MYF. We were on our first official function since arriving in Sibu. At 6 a.m., we gathered at the docks where the river launches docked in Sibu. We were directed to the launch for Mukah. Actually, this was the beginning of one of the most unforgettable twelve-hour boat trip we ever took. We traveled down the Rejang River a short distance, then we turned East into the Igan River. We would continue four or five hours until we arrived at a small river branching to the south. We went a short distance and the launch tied up at the dock at a small village. In fact, it looked like a wide spot in the river and there were four or five shops along the river. Everyone got off and went to look in the shops for something to eat. Fortunately, some of the young people had some food that they shared with us. We ate our lunch on the top deck of the launch.

Since the launch could only navigate during high tide, we waited for the tide to rise. After several hours we resumed our journey. During this phase of the trip, two Chinese boys taught Tom to play Chinese chess. By the third game, he almost beat them. About six p.m., our boat slowed down and moved to the other side of the river. The boat came to a virtual stand still. We saw a small opening in the undergrowth and evidence of a small jetty (dock).

We gathered our gear together to go ashore. There was a large land rover waiting for us. We packed as many as we could into the land rover. Jill and Tom stood between our legs. When everyone was in the truck, they pulled out and we were on our way to Mukah. After two or three minutes I said to Charlotte, "I hear water splashing. Do you hear it?" We turned our heads to the left to look out of the back of the truck. There was only water. We could not see the shore or the coastline. We were driving about 50 feet from the shore in the water. The water was axle deep. Some students saw that we were anxious. They assured us that everything was fine. There was no road at this section of the journey to Mukah so it was necessary to travel on the beach for several miles. Finally, we pulled out of the water onto dry land. An empty bus was waiting for us. We had to wait for the land rover as it returned to the dock to pick up the rest of our group who could not get in the first trip.

Eventually, the others arrived and we began to get on the bus. It was not big enough to hold everyone. After some discussion, we were seated in the bus. Since we were outside of town the decision was made to have those who couldn't get inside to climb on the top of the bus and ride to the corporation limits. There the bus stopped, to let some off and take the rest of us to the destination. The bus returned and picked up the rest of our group.

At this point, our family was in a state of culture shock. We had had an unbelievable trip.

The bus dropped us off in front of a house on the river. There were no streetlights. The night was black except for a crescent moon. We could see only the outline of a house. As we got closer, we saw a raised path on the right leading to the house; it was on stilts five feet above the water. A large log went from the path up to the side door of the house. We had to walk this log over the water for about twenty feet. Jill began to whine. Her mother took her hand and said, "Don't you dare cry." We got into the house safely.

Although it was midnight, the young people prepared some rice and other food to eat. After a service of thanksgiving for the trip, we got our sleeping assignments. Our family was given the only bedroom. There was a bed with no mattress. Boards covered the entire interior of the bed. Straw mats were put over the boards. In that climate, mattresses are too hot, mats remain cool throughout the night.

As we got ready for bed Jill said she had to go to the bathroom. Charlotte asked Su Ming where it was. Su Ming led her to the door and pointed to a small building at the end of a log walk over the river. It was the toilet, 5 feet above the water. As you walked the log you could put your left hand on the side of the house for balance The last twenty feet there was nothing to hold on to. Jill and Charlotte looked at each other. They both went down the log holding onto the house until it ended. Jill went the rest of the way by herself with the flashlight.

The two-day retreat was an unforgettable experience. The adjustments that one was expected to make were a challenge in courage and asserting faith in one's ability to adjust. I am not sure Tom and Jill were aware how resilient they were becoming but we would see them growing over the years in their ability to confront whatever came.

For our children, not only were they taken from their familiar surroundings but placed in situations that would be a challenge to adults. Their resilience would testify to the human spirit's adaptability to change.

The most difficult decision to confront us came in six months. The school year at Sutlive's would soon change since their furlough was to begin in several months. Charlotte and I felt that it was time for Jill and Tom to be enrolled in a local school. After talking this over with Yu Teck Soi, Sibu District Superintendent, I conferred with the principal of the Methodist Primary School. He listened intently to my story and then said he opposed having Western children in the school, because they would take the place of a local young person in the school. He felt the places should be for local children. I did not desire to keep any local youth from going to school. But on the other hand, the issue of Westerners sending their children to boarding school did not appeal to Charlotte or me. He asked me to think about it for several days before we made a final decision.

Two days later, I returned to the principal's office to share with him our decision. Charlotte and I had talked it over, and we had talked to leaders of the church. Those we consulted assured me they did not see how our son and daughter would deprive anyone from entering the school. One of them would speak with the principal on our behalf. After two days, I went to the principal's office to share our decision. I assured him we were determined to have our children educated in the local school. When the school year began, Tom was enrolled in the fourth grade and Jill in the sixth grade.

The school year began with the children anxious about the new school. We knew there would be adjustments that might be difficult to resolve. We believed that the local schools were good for children. We knew that the local school had well-trained teachers and an excellent academic record.

After several weeks, we began to experience the issues which come as one is immersed in a different culture. Chinese classroom discipline is very different from traditional American classrooms. Our kids had a problem with it. When Jill made errors in spelling, her knuckles were hit with a ruler. When Tom needed correction, the teacher twisted his ear.

Tom and Jill were behind in Chinese language study. The other students had been studying Chinese since the first grade. We hired a tutor to help them catch up as much as possible. This went very slowly.

After some weeks had passed, Charlotte had to visit the Methodist Office that was next to the school. It was recess and she noticed that a number of students were gathered around a table; one student was on the table performing some type of antics. It was Tom. She could not tell whether the students were jeering or cheering. She quizzed the kids when they came home and discovered it was both.

Several days after the schoolyard incident, a telephone call came from the Methodist Hostel in Singapore. Betty Snead, the house mother, informed us there would be an opening for two children the next term. They would hold the places open for us for two days. We would have to let her know whether we wanted to send our children.

We were not pleased with what was occurring at the school. The principal's prophecy seemed to be coming true. Besides the discipline in the classes, our hope for a closer relationship between our children and the other children was not evolving as we had hoped. We were both disappointed. We decided to let the kids decide what they would like to do. We asked them that night whether they would like to go to Singapore or stay here. They said, "We thought you would never ask." "Singapore, of course." We immediately called the hostel and confirmed that we wanted the two places for Jill and Tom. Papers were filled out and sent to Betty Snead to complete the school enrollment.

Jill and Tom ready to go the American School in Singapore for the first time.

Before a month passed families gathered at the airport, the Crisologo's, Sutlive's, Root's, and the Shield's and our children. We put them on a plane bound for Singapore. As our fourth grader and sixth grader went through the gates to board the plane, our eyes began to tear up. We both wiped our eyes. We were doing something we said we would never do. Our children had left home. Our lives would never be the same. There would be a place in our life that our children would not be aware of what Mom and Dad experienced. Our work would be like a storybook to be read in a library. Their world would only become sketchily familiar to us in the years to come. Every three months, they came home for a one-week vacation. During a year we would have four weeks together as a family. Charlotte and I felt alone. We were broken-hearted. I was crushed that my efforts with the principal merely fulfilled his prophecy. He knew us better than we knew ourselves. Life goes on and there were other students to teach and lessons to prepare. The time for grief could not be prolonged. Fortunately, our work was consuming and we had little time to sit around feeling sorry for ourselves.

In the years that followed, the period when our children were at home, we parked our responsibilities or duties to make family time the focus of our life together. We tried to get Jill and Tom to share what had been going on at school and at the hostel. Each day new events and experiences were shared with us. If there were any special events or festivals while they were home, we tried to get everyone to go. It was always seven days filled with excitement. For a brief time we shared our lives. The end of the holiday brought the returning ritual of going to the airport and the inevitable tears. All we parents began going out to eat together immediately after the kids left. As we ate we shared our heartbreak at having to send the kids so far away.

Charlotte and I have often discussed the high cost of sending Jill and Tom to Singapore. Perhaps the pain of separation is the cost of seeking to live out the mission God gave to us. After the first three years of school, we never had the experience of helping our kids with their homework. When Tom played in Little League, we were not able to attend the games.

In 1970, we were transferred to Singapore for Jill's last two years of high school and Tom's freshman and sophomore years. These would be a wonderful two years as a family.

In Singapore, we joined a private club for golf and swimming. Charlotte and Jill went swimming and Tom and I played golf. We set every Friday at the Keppel Club for time together. We really could not afford the expensive membership dues, but we were able to trim our expenses so that we could balance our budget.

In Singapore, we attended concerts, school programs and provided cello lessons for Tom. All became part of our family life. Occasionally, we were able to be involved in some homework, but only rarely. During her senior year, Jill took a course in sewing. She chose to made a winter coat that she could wear when we returned to the states the next summer. She became frustrated with the shoulders because they were not coming out correctly. Her mother came to the rescue. Charlotte's tailoring abilities saved the day and the coat was finished and looked very stylish.

As I reflect back over the years in Sarawak and Singapore, I know that I was doing what God wanted me to do. I am not clear that my children's experiences were always positive. I was conscious they had to go along with Dad and Mom as they fulfilled their calling. However, it was not a choice that they made for their lives. I guess children never really have a choice of where they live or go to school. They end up in the location where the parents choose to live and work. In that sense, our life was probably not much different from thousands of other American families. The fact that we lived in a different cultural milieu provided unique experience and situations which Jill and Tom would never have experienced had we not lived in Asia. These experiences have given them unique insights in cross-cultural relationships and communication.

We tried to provide a supportive and loving atmosphere in which our children could grow and develop. As parents, we hope and pray that our life together has enriched and equipped them for the challenges that they will confront in their future.

Charlotte was the director of the Conference MYF Choir for a major canta in Sibu. She is in the center of the first row.

9

Autonomy, Furlough and the Final Decision

In 1968, we were scheduled to return home for a one-year furlough. We arrived in Singapore in transient on the same day that the Constituting Service for the autonomous Methodist Church in Malaysia was occurring. Its establishment brought into existence the vision that had been the dream of our missionary work ever since the arrival of James Hoover, the first missionary to Sarawak, in 1903. Before we left Singapore, we went to the site of the Conference and witnessed the establishment and the commitment service to a continuing ministry of a new Methodist Church. It was inspiring to be present as the mantle was passed and the missionary relationship now took on a new meaning.

We had made arrangements to live in an apartment at The Methodist Theological School in Delaware, Ohio. This would enable us to be centrally located in the state and enable our speaking engagements to be met easily.

The year passed quickly with Jill and Tom enjoying their school. As we made preparations to return to Sarawak, the doctor informed Charlotte that it would be best to have a hysterectomy before we returned to Sarawak. He believed it would be better to have it here in the U.S. than face the possibility of having it during the next term in Sarawak. We made our decision to return by the middle of December and schedules were made to begin our preparations.

In August, 1969, we left for our second term in Sarawak. We knew we were returning to work in an autonomous church. This would mean that we would have a totally different relationship than in the first term. Even though we made every effort in the first term to work with and under Chinese leadership, there was always the unspoken realization that New York controlled the final decisions on the field. This term would be very different.

When we arrived in Sarawak, we were assigned to the same responsibilities we had in the theological school except that I was not the supervisor for the Tulai School. When I left, the church had convinced the government that a local Chinese lay person could do the job effectively. They reached an agreement that enabled this to occur. Charlotte and I celebrated the fact that this had occurred.

One of the immediate decisions that had to be made when we returned was the future of the Chinese Department in the Theological School. Only two students enrolled for the next school year in the entering class. Twelve students were in the other two classes. We had to face the question of whether it was a wise use of resources to keep the Chinese Department open for so few students. Trinity College in Singapore had a Chinese Department to which we could transfer the dwindling Chinese Department. After many heated discussions, the decision was made to close our Chinese Department and transfer the upper class and the entering students to Trinity. This left the question of the appointment of the faculty. Arrangements were made for one of the Chinese members of the faculty to transfer to Trinity and I would move to Trinity to be in charge of the Field Education Program. Charlotte would be assigned after we arrived in Singapore.

Trinity Theological School in Singapore. Graduates and faculty in 1971.

A typical market scene in Singapore or even in Sarawak.

The next two years in Singapore raised many questions in my mind about the need for foreign missionaries in an autonomous church. The church was now self-supporting, self-sustaining and self-governing. Should not the faculty training the clergy be local national leaders? Field education where students get practical training in parish administration and program, should be done by a Chinese. Since ours was to be a three-year term, we made the decision that our two years in Singapore would bring to a close this chapter of our life. It was a hard decision because we had made a commitment for our life's work to be in mission. We had learned to speak Mandarin fluently. We loved our relationships with the Chinese community among whom we lived and worked. For months we agonized over this new crossroad in our lives. After months of indecision, we finally wrote to the Board of Global Ministries and the annual Conference in the United States that we would terminate our missionary service at the end of our term in two years.

I felt it would be easier to adjust if I did not go back to my home conference. Therefore, I wrote to a District Superintendent in Indiana who had been pastor of one of our supporting churches. He immediately sent a reply that they would welcome us to the North Indiana Conference. He had an appointment for us. All that had to be done was to get my Bishop in Ohio to agree to transfer me to their conference. In 1964, I had transferred my membership when we arrived in Sarawak to the Sarawak Chinese Conference. When autonomy was ratified in 1968, I transferred my membership back to my home conference in Ohio. The bishop would not release me to the North Indiana Conference. I appealed to the personnel office in our Board to intervene to convince the bishop to transfer me. I explained the reason I wanted to transfer. After three months of conversations and a number of letters to the bishop, no one was able to get him to change his mind. I had no choice but to return to Ohio. In 1972, when our term was up we left for the United States. It was the middle of June. The Annual Conference was over and I had not been notified of my appointment. When we left Singapore for home, we had no idea where we would serve when we got home. I wrote my mother a letter to see if she had heard where we were appointed. When we arrived in Toledo and were on our way to my mothers' home, she told us that her pastor had found out that we were appointed to the First United Methodist Church in Zanesville, Ohio. I looked up the church and its membership and salary; I was shocked. I discovered that my salary would be lower than when we were missionaries. The church was at the level of the first appointment of a clergy after graduation from a theological school. This ignited something in my heart and spirit that I did not need at this point. I was furious.

After we moved into the parsonage and met with the District Superintendent, the reason for the appointment was clear. The bishop considered my time with the Board of Missions of little relevance to parish work in the U.S. Since I had stepped out of line and left the conference, I had to begin at the beginning if I wished to return. When I heard this, the anger in my heart only grew. If he felt this way, why did he not release me to Indiana where they felt my experience would make a valuable contribution. No one could answer my questions. Finally the experience of returning to Ohio came to a head in December, 1972. I was attending a seminar on Bible Study led by our bishop. During one of our informal breaks I was standing next to him and introduced myself to him. He commented, "Oh yes, you were in China." I interrupted to explain that we had in fact had been in Sarawak and Singapore. He then commented that it is really almost impossible to transfer any of your experience there to work in the United States. I abruptly turned and walked to another part of the room. I finished my coffee and as I resumed my seat, my insides were in turmoil. At this point I noticed that all the District Superintendents were persons I had known for 20 years. Not one of them had come to welcome me back into the fellowship. I would learn later that they were too embarrassed to speak to me because of the appointment.

The next six months were a time of personal turmoil and anger. My anger grew. I finally called the Board of Missions to see if resources were available for me to study for a PhD. They informed me that there was no help available. I called Boston University and spoke to my theological school about the possibility of working on a doctorate. They were encouraging. At the end of my first year back in the States I received a letter from a college classmate who was president of a United Methodist College in Michigan. He informed me of the opportunity to apply to be the chaplain at their university. I eagerly sent my resume. By return mail he notified me that he was sorry, but they could not consider me for the job. It was necessary to have a Ph.D. Everywhere I turned, I seemed to find a door slammed in my face. Finally that Fall I noted an opening in the National division of our Mission Board and I decided to apply for the position. By this time, I had become aware that I actually had Native American roots. My family had hidden this for many years. When I applied in 1973, I was told that the position was for a minority and I would not qualify for consideration. I was furious. How did they know I was not a minority? They never asked. They had no record of my ancestry. Suffice it to say more fuel was poured on my anger.

In 1974, the Conference attempted to move me to a new appointment. They called at least a dozen times trying to rectify the embarrassing situation they had created for me and for them. Tom was a senior at the Zanesville high school. I would not ask him to move his senior year. It was important for him to have his final year without being uprooted again.

The next year would be an eventful year in our Zanesville church. We were developing a unique inner city program that we called the Pierce St. Community. Under Charlotte's leadership and my supportive involvement, our program grew. Over 600 children were involved in our daily program after school. It was a challenge that called on our experience at Farm Camp, Work Camps and our overseas encounters. The program grew and became a vital program in the District and in the Conference. By the end of the second year, we arranged to have a young Black minister appointed to our staff to be the assistant director under my leadership. All the time my anger was unabated. Not only did I feel unappreciated. I was humiliated.

The next year, the conference persuaded me to accept an appointment to a large congregation in Dayton, Ohio. We accepted the opportunity and found ourselves in a challenging environment. Three years later, I applied for a job with the American Friends Service Committee in Dayton. I was hired and left the church at the end of three years. My anger was still driving me. I was seeking something but didn't seem to know what. I was the Executive Secretary for the Ohio Region for two years. During this period we took a weekend to journey to Boston for interviews to investigate a Ph.D. After two years, I asked for an appointment to a congregation in the conference. I was appointed to Hope United Methodist Church in Whitehouse, near Toledo. I was elated because it was near my mother's home.

My inner life did not improve. I had come to the conclusion that perhaps I needed to seek a job not in the church. I contacted Haldane, a service that helps an individual evaluate his employment and clarify goals. I made an appointment to get the information about their resources. After some discussion, Charlotte and I decided that it would be worth the $3000 fee. I enrolled in the program. From the first, this appeared to be just what I needed. The individual who worked with me had a ministerial background. With his guidance, I began to explore my commitments, my goals and my vision and purpose in life. By the time I had finished the program, it was clear that I was exactly at the place God wanted me to be. Somewhere along the way I had lost my passion. I discovered that it was only pushed to the background. I needed to feel again the rush of passion that comes with proclaiming the good news of God's love and the wonderful gift of life.

It was at this point that my anger began to subside. I began to feel a new sense of mission and purpose. It was during the second year of our ministry in Whitehouse that my mother died. The church gave us tremendous support. They insisted that Charlotte and I attend a Koinonia Retreat. It was an ecumenial retreat movement that had grown out of the Roman Catholic Cruciel Retreat movement. Reluctantly, we agreed to take a weekend to share in the retreat. It would be a tremendous spiritual experience that lifted me out of my depression after my mother's death. But also, it would be the final door through which I would go through in rediscovering my own mission and purpose in life. It was in the quiet silence and expectant listening that I would experience again the presence of God in a powerful way in my deepest inner sanctum. I had reclaimed the passion that Bonhoeffer had ignited in my heart so many years before. Peace had once again became a major concern in my own ministry and life. It was from this retreat that Charlotte I again found each other at a depth we had once known. Somewhere along the way I had apparently allowed anger to push everything I loved away. Unconsciously, I had been destroying my own life as well as the life of those I loved.

It is amazing to me how often we clergy do not allow lay persons to minister to us. But in Whitehouse, I was open and receptive to the ministry some of the congregation sought to offer to me. Their love, patience, and insight became the source of new birth and a renewed life. Fortunately, I was open to their ministry and through them I was again brought close to the Creative Spirit who rules life and He once again touched my life in a miraculous way. I felt whole for the first time since we returned from Sarawak.

BACK FROM BORNEO

10

In Search of My Roots

I learned from the Chinese to be proud of my heritage. Their identity as a person was rooted in their heritage. Not only were they Chinese but they were of a specific group of Chinese, i.e. Foochows, Cantonese, Hunanese, etc. They belonged to a group that gave them roots and pride. Previously, I had never given much thought to my own heritage. When I returned from Asia, I began to look seriously at my own roots. I discovered that my grandmother was a half breed. Her mother was a full-blooded Narragansett Indian.

This Pow-Wow was my first in-depth introduction to my own heritage. Our leader was a Choctaw from Michigan, and his wife was a Navajo. The first experience they offered us was prayer time at the opening ceremony. Our leader took a shell, put in sweet grass and then lit it. He used a feather to fan the grass so it would burn. The smoke would carry to each of us the gift of the Spirit of the Elders. As he went around the circle, each person was enveloped by smoke on his head, down his back and up his side. Each of us were enveloped by the prayers. He opened for me a door that would lead on a journey of self-discovery. It would expand my understanding of life. He shared, after the smudging, his insights on the significance of an individual. He said, "Only the individual person can make the journey for himself. No one can make the journey for you."

As the Pow Wow unfolded, the power of individual choice became clearly the foundation of the journey. As other Cherokees and Navajos shared their experiences at sweat lodges, a new understanding of myself began to emerge.

I truly was an individual who had the responsibility to commence the journey to self-understanding.

This insight would be a compelling power to guide my pilgrimage to selfhood. I came to understand that each person is a unique living being placed on earth to touch, experience and to learn. This is the advice of the Elders who have shared their wisdom over the centuries. One of the most powerful forces in the life of each individual is the sense of worth which each is given at birth. Self-worth and personal dignity is birthed in love and wholeness as we enter into a family. (tribe)

The understanding one has of his identity determines the nature of the journey he travels in life. In both the secular and religious world, attacks against self-worth have occurred for centuries. It is a rare experience to hear that humankind is good. Rarer still is to hear that people are of infinite worth. We might hear this in words; but in deeds, we seldom experience it. I believe it is one of the essential ingredients in life.

Since I was reared in Western Christian civilization, I was taught the universal guilt which is believed to be at the heart of created life. Through mythologies, I learned that people have been sinners since the beginning of time. This view brought me to the beginning of the twenty-first century with a perverted view of my self-worth and the worth of others. This particular perception had been taught in a manner that it explained away personal responsibility and did not affirm the ability of humankind to be a determiner of it's own destiny.

I have spent much of my life within a traditional Christian church. Therefore, I tend to explain the world as sinful. As with most people, I found myself mentally addicted to the idea of sin. I could not detach myself from it. Many thinkers imply that this is why sin is a universal fact—its pervasive nature. We have been told it is one of the undeniable facts of life.

In one discussion group in which I participated, there was unanimous agreement that there has been an assault on the self-worth of the individual. We often shared how for each of us, our own sense of personhood has been depreciated and how we have minimized the significance of our individuality. Immediately, we would turn to sin as one of the answers in our discussion. Certainly, self-worth is important; however, we cannot escape the fact of sin, several reminded us.

It should be noted that the emphasis on sin is a concept put forth by the Apostle Paul. This was not a theme in Jesus' teachings. Everywhere Paul preached, he called people to repent and turn away from their sinful lives. He spoke out of the depth of his own personal experience. This was the story of his own life. Jesus, on the other hand, gathered people together by the sea and on the hillside to share with them the fact that they were "light", the "salt", the bearers of love. He called people to love others as you love yourselves, not out of repentance or disgust of one's life, but because you love yourself you can love others. It is in discovering what "love of one's self" means that we understand the love we are called to share.

Christians have been taught that caretaking of those around them is a virtue. Whether a member of the family or the poor in the community, people are approached as those who are in need of help. The person who approaches them has a sense that they have the understanding and insight that will enable the other person to come to terms with sin. Whether this is in our local community or on the distant shores of an another country, people feel the same powerful urge to care for others. Many envision themselves as rescuers. As I look around the world, I sense that other people need others to be there for them. They attach themselves to others. People feel compelled to help the other person.

When I attend church, I hear that we have a responsibility for others. This responsibility is interpreted to mean that I am to step in and interpose myself into the needy person's life. As I have observed people who become more involved with others, they often become obsessed with the anxiety of others. They are driven to pity and guilt over the problems others are confronting.

When a person's sense of personal worth begins to fade, his low self-esteem is obvious. He begins to blame himself for everything. He observes the affluence around him and what it is doing to the poor. One begins to feel guilty about what he has or wants from life. He blames himself for not being more sensitive to the needs of others. I have observed that people seeking to serve others often become angry, self-righteous, and indignant when others blame and criticize people. We hear people say, "If others had the concern which I have the world would not be as it is today."

Underneath the bravado is a person who is frightened because he is not good enough. He finds himself taking everything personally. He feels like a victim. He feels guilty about everything that occurs. He expects himself to do everything perfectly. When it does not happen, he is devastated.

Underneath the emerging personality with low self-esteem is a framework that enables the individual so to interpret his understanding of life that his living is filled with superficial feelings of worth that he gets from helping others. He looks at others and begins to hope that good things would begin to happen to him. He might begin to convince himself that he doesn't deserve happiness. This is what he has given up in order to help others. He settles for being needed by others.

Native American spirituality asserts that life begins in loneliness and ends in relationships. Creation, which birthed humankind with dignity and worth, is frustrated by the human quest I have described. One thing all people possess equally is their loneliness.

Because of the expansion of life, we are aware of the source of our misery and unhappiness. Love, hate, greed and generosity are all rooted within our loneliness—within our desire to be needed and loved. The only way we can overcome our loneliness is through touching. People have to get close to others. This is the only way they can learn to be a total being. Touch is essential for mental health and good vibes between human beings.

Touch is the subject of a chapter in Dean Ornish's book *LOVE AND SURVIVAL*:the scientific basis for the healing power of intimacy. I want to lift out a significant insight in his book.[1]

"We are touchy-feely creatures. We are creatures of community. Those individuals, societies, and cultures who learned to take care of each other, to love each other, and to nurture relationships with each other during the past several thousand years were more likely to survive than those who did not. Those people who did not learn to take care of each other often did not make it. In our culture, the idea of spending time taking care of each other and creating communities has become increasingly rare. Ignoring these ideas imperils our survival."

This quotation lifts up one of the most important aspects of life and relationships. Everyone of us lives in relationship to someone. There are occasions when we negate or belittle one or more of our relationships. The existence of a relationship is directly related to the nearness of the other person. If people are kept at a distance, a significant relationship is not possible and perhaps no relationship actually exists. Relationship by its very nature implies a closeness to the other. Therefore, touch is crucial to it. When I am in a position to experience touch, I become aware that some persons are very uncomfortable. The one-on-one contact that is necessary for life often causes some people to pull away and move in the other direction, but it is in touching that spontaneity can enter into a relationship with others. Spontaneity is so often based on the overcoming of one's own inhibitions and feelings about relationships with people. I might feel like hugging someone, but I seek to control the spontaneous expression because I do not know how the other person will react.

I am concerned about the person who may find my spontaneity uncomfortable. We are often unable to reach out and touch or be touched in a moment of joyful expression. Joy and elation result from such a sharing of the experience of the moment. For some persons it is the natural result of a feeling of joy. For others touching is a moment of terror.

This brings us to another dimension of the *loneliness* that is a common denominator of all people. Boundaries and feelings of privacy are deeply involved in our loneliness. All of us are surrounded by boundaries. We are fearful when someone reaches across to touch them. I have seen a person visibly shake and pull away when someone reaches out to touch him. Why? I am not sure I have an

---

1. Ornish, Dean, LAS, p. 12.

answer. What is important is a respect for the other person. Must they share the same feeling of spontaneity that another wishes to express? At the same time, how can one honor the very real feelings of the other person who is led to express herself through touch? To turn away from a person merely because she does not express herself in the same manner as I do is no excuse for exclusion of another from the circle of life. Not only is room for both on the circle, but the circle is incomplete without either.

How do we deal with the issue of touch? For some there are sexual overtones in touching, or stroking of another person. Granted, that might not be the intention of the instigator of the expression but it is the feeling of many people in such a situation. This gives a false interpretation to what is occurring. Yet, the person's feeling in both cases is very valid. One may be an incorrect interpretation, but the message that I receive during such an encounter is not the one that is sent by the instigator.

The Importance of Touch

I asked myself if the problem is me? Is the problem in the other person? I believe we both bring to the moment the experience of the years. For one it is a life that has been devoid of touching. Expressions of intimacy have been few, yet they have evolved ways of expressing intimacy over the years. For the other, a whole different set of experiences may have become part of her life. Many are able to express it in the confines of their own home. In the intimacy of their own bedroom they have found a haven in which they feel safe and secure enough to express themselves through touching. For the other, touch has been an intimate and normal part of the experience of life. Wherever one finds human relationships, touching is one of the warm and compassionate expressions a person encounters. People grow comfortable with this type of intimacy. This type of person has few inhibitions about expressing how he feels about others. Touch is as natural as breathing.

As people have become socialized in American culture, we have come to have a secularized and one-dimensional understanding of reality. The dominant worldview in our time flows from the scientific and technological revolution of the last few centuries. Americans have a difficult time grasping the sense of the relatedness or connectedness to Creation. We have been reared in a culture that divides and splits life into many segments.

Native Americans have a different perception of the world. Their perception is of a Great Harmony at the heart of Creation. Whether it is animals, birds, trees, rocks, mountains, all have an innate relationship to this Harmony—all except humankind. Humankind is a determiner. Humans can be made whole only through learning of the Harmony. Humankind must experience the spirit of the universe if a person is to understand. This encounter conveys the experience and presence of the Great Harmony. Learning what wholeness means is crucial to living life. This suggests another insight I have gleaned from experience-**all life is connected.** This understanding is grounded in one's sense of personhood. Wholeness is rooted in love, and most of all, people are called to love. We must care for others and be a part of something greater than ourselves.

It is obvious that one of the ingredients of a fulfilled life is self-respect and self-worth. It is where we begin if we hope to have a world of varied textures. Therefore, it is at the personal level where we begin to build a foundation that will anchor love and peace deep into the life of humankind.

Our notions of happiness are wedded to human connections. Isolation, exile, loneliness, and despair mark tragic endings in life. We have become suspicious of communal images that appear as perfect portraits of beaming families around the dinner table or other Madison Avenue images that ring hollow. We respond with cynical smiles. Even young people understand the desire for community and what Carl. G. Jung called the participation mystique—a group undertow that demands conformity at any cost. In adolescence, we had our first experience of community in cliques, which either included us or excluded us with rigid requirements that we dress, talk, and act like the group.

We entered the workplace and discovered we had to adapt to absurd organizational realities if we wanted to be part of the community. Occasionally, we were able to do more than yearn for community—we experienced it. A sense of shared meaning and joy in working harmoniously with others occasionally emerged.

Consciousness of the forces that connect us is intrinsically spiritual. Our actions are directed by neither a boss nor majority rule. Rather, we are directed by subtle energies that we feel by cultivating a quiet kind of inner listening. As we express our abilities as individuals, we also participate in community and we tap into the natural rhythm of others in a way that coordinates with our own rhythm and actions.

"Different Drums and Different Drummers"[2]

If I do not want what you want, please try not to tell me that my want is wrong. Or if I believe other than you, at least pause before you correct my view.

---

2. Keirsey,D., PLEASE UNDERSTAND ME, p.1

Or if my emotion is less than yours, or more, given the same circumstances, try not to ask me to feel more strongly or weakly.
Or yet if I act, or fail to act, in the manner of your design for action, let me be.
I do not, for the moment at least, ask you to understand me. That will come only when you are willing to give up changing me into a copy of you.
I may be your spouse, your parent, your offspring, your friend, or your colleague. If you will allow me any of my own wants, or emotions, or beliefs or actions, then you open yourself, so that some day these ways of mine might not seem so wrong, and might finally appear to you as right—for me.
To put up with me is the first step to understanding me. Not that you embrace my ways as right for you, but that you are no longer irritated or disappointed with me for my seeming waywardness. And in understanding me you might come to prize my differences from you, and, far from seeking to change me, preserve and even nurture those differences.

We must remind ourselves that each individual has a will, a heart, a mind and a soul. It is essential in all of our relationships that we remember that what is true of ourselves is also true of every person.

We must awaken to the slumbering destructive force at the heart of humankind's current journey. By acknowledging what isn't working, what is demeaning, fruitless, boring, disappointing and empty about work and life, we will identify the darkness and the negative in our lives so that we will be empowered to move beyond them.

The old view that the universe is a great machine is dead. Today, *we understand that the universe is an organism.* Consequently, our life must be organic in all its aspects—work, education, family, and will spring from the inner, hidden mystery and creativity. We must connect all that we are and do to the Creative Power of the universe.

Previously science taught that matter is composed of inert atoms. Today, science has enabled us to understand that atoms are structures bursting with activity in fields of energy. *Creation and life are an ever-changing choreography filled with wonder.*

During the eighteenth, nineteenth and early twentieth centuries humankind believed that the earth was composed of dead things. Therefore, people had no need to worry about the impact of their actions on the earth. People saw the great resources of nature as finite in both use and value. They were driven to exploit the vast richness of the earth. By the end of the 20th century humankind understands that the earth is not a dead, but a living organism. It is constantly birthing life and expanding the reaches of life. Humankind has an obligation to honor the earth, not by exploitation and destruction, but by nurture, gentleness and compassion. The moral implication of our relationship to the earth is more profound than anyone anticipated.

Some people believe that everything is predetermined. Life is expected to follow a predictable pattern. In many aspects of life, people often perceive that boredom dominates. In order to spur human creativity it is often necessary to have ever-increasing rewards to keep people working. It has become obvious that freedom and spontaneity exist. As life expands its reaches of creativity and spontaneity, people have begun to discover a sense of meaning in their efforts to live and relate to a vibrant, ever-changing world.

Relationships are the key to the meaning of a life. They are essential to our self-worth and selfhood. Each one of us is essential in the search for truth and knowledge. Every individual is an aspect of the creative gift of life. There are positive affirmations about life that I discovered that have been the basis of relationships on the journey.

Affirmations Of The Journey

The **first affirmation** is so obvious I hesitate to list it. We must allow other people to be who they are as persons. We cannot remake others into the image we would like them to mirror. People are not clay for us to mold into forms pleasing to our sight.

The **second affirmation** is that People are ends, not means. Yes, the differences are upsetting at times, and pleasing at other times. We do not always concur with the choices others make in life, yet it is their choices that make them unique. Why should they conform to our idea of what their life should be?

The **third affirmation** is that The Circle of Creation asserts that every life and point of view is unique. Beware when you seek to tamper with it. It is not for you to adjust it. It is a life that has been given and it must now follow its own path. Most of all, the person must discover for himself the path which he must follow on the journey.

This creates anxiety for others who long to see the person be what they envision she can become in life. Yet the vision of another is not necessarily the vision that one has perceived for one's self. Parents have a continual struggle to respect the uniqueness of their children. It never ends. They always seem to have a vision or a goal for their child that is not always the same as the child has for herself. The struggle of parents is with the idea that "I know what is best for her. I only want her to be happy. I only want to help her find success." It is true, this is what parents want for their children. Is one capable of determining for others what they need and ought to achieve in life? If parents could only find the wisdom to relate as one who is concerned and supportive, the rift that often develops between children and parents could be avoided. It is when parents try to impose their own view on the child that a rupture in relationships occur. Who wants someone else to make decisions about what he does with his life?

I cannot stress enough the truth and power contained in the Circle of Life. Each person is born on the Circle. They have been born at a single spot on the circle. No one has or will ever view life from that special spot. To grasp its truth is to grab hold of the power of Life and to allow the Creative Process of life to direct one's days.

We strive to ascertain what it is we can change and what we cannot change. This was one aspect of life my mother exemplified. This was her favorite prayer.

> *"God, grant me the serenity to accept the things I cannot change; The courage to change the things I can: And the wisdom to know the difference."*

Every morning she prayed this prayer. Her life was directed by a peaceful acceptance of others that led to relationships of positive encounters. Never did she interpose into my life about any decision that I had made or was about to make. She listened and affirmed my decisions. Whether she agreed with it or not, I will never know. I cannot remember one instance when she ever said, "You should not do that." My father followed closely this style of parenting. Sure, there were times when it was necessary to say something about my behavior, but it was not said in a way that I felt belittled or scolded for what I had done. They always helped me to understand the implications of what I had chosen to do in that instance. I am sure they did not agree with many of the choices I made in my life. Yet, they saw their role to be one of supporting, loving, and touching. As Dr. Ruth Turrell, one of our psychologist friends commented one time about rearing children, we should be 'under', 'with' and 'for', not 'at', 'on' and 'against'. Even though my parents did not know the formula she gave us, they followed it in our family. It should be a guide for all of us in our relationships as parents, husbands, wives, friends or children.

People who have lost the sense of their identity also lose their sense of relatedness to nature. They lose the capacity to feel empathy for animals and other forms of life. My wife was in charge of a program in one community that had a day care program as part of their activities. During Holy Week, there was a special program for the children. On this particular day they had brought in baby ducks for the children to see, and touch. The children were excited and thrilled. For many of them this was the first time they had ever seen or touched a real baby duck. As they were returning to their rooms, they were permitted to carry one of the baby ducks back to the room if they wished. One three-year-old boy picked up one of the ducks. As they were going down the steps to their room, he put his finger and thumb around the neck of the duck so tightly he squeezed the neck together. The head of the duck popped off and blood spurted on the wall. I have wondered over the years what has happened to that young child?

11

The Elders Speak

The drums began to beat. Everyone gathered for the evening festivities. In the center of the circle were five young men beating on the drum. One sang. I had been to Pow Wow's before, but never noticed the details. I didn't understand any of the words, but felt the call to prayer and the gathering of persons into a community of joy and sharing. As the drums became muffled for a few moments, one of the Elders began to explain what would happen tonight. He moved into the circle and began to dance. He invited everyone to join the dance. During this early stage of the evening, I had a memorable experience. Immediately after he started to dance, I tried to get the rhythm of the drum beat. I am not very musical and could not hear it. I closed my eyes and bowed my head. My arms were on my knee, my head bowed, holding my chin in the palm of my hands. I listened intently to the beat. Deep inside I began to feel the beat. It was as if it were beating in rhythm with my heart. All at once in my mind I saw a circle where people were dancing. They danced for joy with great energy. The fire obscured their faces and smoke gave an eerie feeling to the event. I felt as if I was in the center dancing and celebrating the event at that moment. I am not sure how long my head was bowed, but all of sudden after several quick beats of the drum I opened my eyes to witness the end of the dance.

Reflecting on this vision during the weekend it became clear that I had had the privilege to be with the elders. They had led me As I reflected on this vision during the weekend, it became clear that I had had the privilege to be with the elders. They had led me to a new awareness of mysef. Strangely, up to this point in my life Elders were not especially significant. As I thought, it became clear that I had missed one of the great learnings in life. Elders have much to share with us, Their wisdom and understanding of life unlocks many doors to understanding. It was at this point I became open to what was being shared and experienced.

Native Americans speak of the four powers that play a crucial role in our growing to self-hood. Non-Indians do not normally lift them up for consideration. Let me briefly share what I have come to understand these powers mean in my life.

We all live our lives in the lodge of our bodies, our minds and our hearts. The Circle is given to us as a way of touching. It is a way of experiencing our harmony with every other living thing around us. It is a reminder of the wholeness of life and creation. Our life is part of all that surrounds us. If we view life from one perspective, we will only have a partial view.

In the early 1950's, we were at a retreat in New England with the Young Friends from Cambridge, Massachusetts. On Sunday morning eight of us, along with our hosts, Mr. and Mrs. Barrett met in the town library to share in a meeting for worship. What occurred that morning during worship has left an indelible impression on my life.

Worship began in traditional Quaker silence. As we centered down, a quiet stillness pervaded our meeting. I felt a sense of warmth surrounding me as the meeting progressed. A constant stream of scripture verses were moving through my mind. They slowed and one became a sharp focus for my meditation. In meditation, its meaning and impact began to become clear to my mind and spirit; someone in the group quoted that same passage of scripture. He shared insights that had emerged in his listening. Silence again became moments of expectation. After about ten minutes, someone began to lead in an old familiar hymn. Everyone joined in the refrain. When the song ended we again waited in silence for further evidence of the Divine Presence. When the time came to adjourn the meeting everyone shook hands. We sat in the circle for a few minutes and shared the experiences of the hour together. One after another commented that he was thinking of the same scripture that was shared with the meeting. Likewise, the song was in every mind when the person began to sing. Coincidence? Maybe, but I doubt it. This mystical experience which claimed our worship that Sunday morning enabled each person to have a personal vision of God's movement into each of our lives. This became for me the leading vision of God for my journey—very personal and very real. This was and is the source of my religious commitment and direction. This is where I have gone in my moments of despair and confusion to find hope.

A similar truth has been at the heart of my discoveries in Native American spirituality. It is the personal vision of each person on the quest that brings the experience of truth and purpose. This is a uniquely personal experience. Unique, in that it comes to a single individual with a single purpose and meaning. The quest in life finds its direction in each individual life. So it is with each of us. We must discover our own vision, our own truth, and our own journey.

Black Elk's vision has helped me to see how life has unity and a sense of direction.[1] Life has given wisdom for my own journey. I would like to share it with each you so that you might understand the nature of the journey that I have experienced.

The first power he refers to is that which is in the **North**. It is **wisdom**. Its color is white and the animal medicine is the buffalo. One who views life with the gift of the North will be a wise person. However, he will be a cold person without feeling. His knowledge and wisdom will be separated from the rest of life that is so necessary for wholeness.

The second power is the **South** that is green. It represents **innocence**. The gift of the South is a gift of trust. Its animal is the mouse. A person with this gift sees everything up close. His vision is limited to the immediate world. While he can gather many things, he is unable to understand all that he has seen and gathered. He is too close to the ground and too near-sighted to see anything except what is right in front of him.

The third power is the **West**, **introspection**. The color is Black and the animal is the Bear. Those who possess only the gift of the West will go over the same thought again and again. They will always be undecided.

The fourth power is the **East**. It is **illumination**. The color is gold and the animal is the Eagle. Those who live only in the East will have a clear and far-sighted vision of the Eagle, but he will never be close to things. This person will feel separated, high above life, and will never understand or believe that he can be touched by anything.

The person who seeks to live life fully and with wholeness will travel in all four directions and utilize each of the four powers. They will give us insight into our direction and the way of continuing our journey.

One of the major themes of the four powers is that life is a whole. Because of our experiences, we find this difficult to understand. We discover very early in life that there is an estrangement that seems to dominate. We need to be reminded that man is a whole.

The Four Powers suggested to me new insights for living life. The idea that there is a harmony to life and a unity that includes all of creation has helped me

---

1. Neihardt, John C., *Black Elk Speaks.* University of Nebraska Press, Lincoln and London. 1979. 298 pp. The author has not given specific quotes but has made every effort to convey the thought and meaning of the four powers.

understand the connectedness of all life. The idea that there is an eternal war within creation and that the battle between good and evil threatens to destroy life has dominated much of the thinking of church people. The four powers suggest that life is a positive and growing force with harmony at its core.

Another teaching of the Elders is that we cannot be detached from life. We are connected. We are involved in the Creative Process. Even if we are passive, we are involved by our passivity. Creation makes no allowance for any aspect of the Creative Process to be unresponsive and outside of its power and creativity. The isolation which dominated the past millenium is not a part of the reality of Creation. It was an invention of the mind of men to explain something that they did not understand.

As I look back at this chapter and the previous chapter, I begin to sense the many threads that lead to selfhood. Loss of selfhood is the most destructive event that can occur in the life of a person. There are many who confront us on our life's journey who would stop us from going North, or prevent us from going West, or impede our journey to the East or propel us to the South. In any event the journey is perilous. When we discover the harmony of the four powers and the harmony of the Creative Process, life can move with the silence of the breeze and the strength of the oak.

As soon as I begin to get comfortable with an insight and think I finally understand, something comes along to upset the balance I have achieved. One Sarawak experience illustrates how we continually find ourselves challenged to rethink our selfhood and our personal mission in life.

The thin, white strip through the jungle was hardly visible from the main road. Tze-jen climbed up behind me on the motorcycle and we were off into the dense undergrowth before us. We plunged into a mass of bushes behind which might be a wall, a mountain, or a river. But, quickly the path emerged before us as we made our way through the thicket.

I followed the narrow cement path winding between trees and over dark streams, thinking back ten years to the night in Cincinnati and the packed church. The speaker, from the Methodist Board of Missions, spoke on the challenge of Southeast Asia. His words still rang in my ears.

"Millions of people face the inevitability of starvation unless the world rises to the occasion. Unless the developed nations of the world harness their resources and put on a massive program of development, the world is doomed. Mothers and children, fathers and sons have no future. As the wars tear apart one country in Asia after another, only suffering and starvation are the certainties of life. Three-fourths of the world will go to bed hungry tonight and will get up tomorrow morning still unsatisfied, while here in America, affluence takes over in every life. Enough food is thrown away in an average home daily to feed a family in Asia for five or six days. Here we sit as comfortable, middle class, persons with secure futures. The need is for people with expertise. Leadership needs to be trained. Development cannot take place until the skilled technicians are available to contribute their talents for the sake of humanity. Church after church in Asia suffers from a need for leadership."

"Wow! That was close." I just avoided hitting a tree stump jutting out into the path. The sun was now warmer and the air more oppressively humid. Ten years ago was a world away. Expertise, development, leadership-ran through my mind; that night as I was challenged to give my life for a mission in a foreign land.

Here I am with a B.A. from Ohio Wesleyan University, a M.Div. from Boston University, and a certificate from Yale University for Chinese competence-ten years experience as a pastor. Who would have thought that a speech would revolutionize my whole life? "Dau le."[2] Tse-jen hopped off and headed toward the dingy, white building. I turned around to go back for another passenger so Sunday School could get started. I turned to retrace the way I had come and went a little faster with no rider; the path was drying rapidly for the sun was scorching. In minutes, I was back at the main road. "Who's next?" Ai-ming stepped up and slid onto the Honda behind me. Again we set forth on the path through the underbrush and forged our way through the ferns and tall grass toward our destination two miles in the jungle—a small building with a cross over the door.

Again I recalled a professor in theological school reminding us that many pastors often become involved with mimeographing, waxing floors, emptying trash and arranging classrooms. He reminded us that our education prepared us for other responsibilities than such tasks. "Find some laymen who could keep those things in order. Keep yourselves free for the more important tasks which only a well-trained person can fulfill." "Oh, what a mess," I commented as we hit a patch of slippery mud-the front wheel wiggled to and fro but finally I got the motorcycle under control; I hit the throttle, Ai-ming held on tighter, and we were on our way. "Don't do the mundane tasks."

The conferences I had attended in Hong Kong, New Delhi, Ceylon, Washington D.C. and New York flashed through my mind. The brilliant theological insights that occupied each meeting were all to help us enable the church to be relevant to the world. What is relevance? The motorcycle roared out—relevance, relevance, relevance, relevance, re-. "Here we are," I shouted over the roar of the

2. Chinese meaning "we have arrived".

engine! As I stopped in front of the church, I let Ai-ming off, then went back on the same road for another passenger. This time the motorcycle sped over the path at forty miles per hour. In minutes I was back at the road. "Who's next," I asked. George, a six foot, Chinese gentleman got on and we sped off into the jungle. Not the unknown jungle, but the relevant. Relevance was still on my mind. Is what I'm doing now, roaring through the jungle on a motorcycle transporting people to a non-descript little building in a jungle clearing to hold a service, relevant? Couldn't someone else do this? Why should I be doing this? Five years of post-graduate study and I am now the driver for a group of students on their field work assignment from the theological school. Is this what is meant by being a servant? "We're here!" George, my colleague climbed off. Jokingly the students cried out, "Who's next?"

12

The Great Illusion

WALKING THE PATH WITH JOY

Source of Sound: in the roar and the whisper,
in the breeze and the whirlwind, a Name is heard.
Order springs into existence
as arms reach out to embrace all creation.
Unite the crowd within
in a vision of passionate purpose:
light mates with form.
Help fulfill what lies within the circle of life:
each day no more, no less.
Untangle the knots within so that with mended hearts
there may be simple ties to others.
Deceived neither by the outer nor the inner-
free to walk the path with joy.
Truly-power to these statements-may they be the ground
from which all actions grow: Sealed in trust and faith Amen![1]

I threw myself into the chair totally oblivious to everything around me. I was absolutely stunned. I shook my head and couldn't believe what the doctor had

---

1. The Lord's Prayer is a translation by the author from the Aramaic. I was guided by the book *Prayers of the Cosmos* by Neil Douglas-Klotz. It is available from the Abwoon Study Circle, Box 361655, Milpitas, CA 95036. The Aramaic language is the one that Jesus spoke when he taught and conversed in his day. If there is an original language in which to cast his teachings it would be Aramaic, not Greek or Hebrew.

said. "You have heart trouble. Your aortic valve is damaged. You must not mow the yard or do anything with exertion," the doctor had said. I felt that I was standing in the center of an intersection waiting for a semi-truck to come roaring at me at any moment. BOOM! It could all be over!

Control is an illusion I wanted to believe was true. However, I had to admit I could not control life. Everyone wants to believe that he is in control of his life. We can make decisions that matter. We want to believe we can help others to change into the persons we would like them to become. In one sense, it is good to help people. We do believe that each of us wants to have meaning in our life. We do not want to waste our life. We know that life can really bring great joy and satisfaction to a person who discovers how to live a meaningful life. Of course, the important issue is "What is meant by meaning?". It is here that Jesus can be a guide for us. He did not teach a formula for living. Rather, he taught that there is an experience at the heart life that transforms a person's focus and purpose from self to others. Therein is the secret key that unlocks the meaning at the heart of life. This, Jesus believed, comes from discovering sacrificial love (agape).

Unfortunately, many people end up hoping to change their lives and others' with defined doctrines and rigid belief systems. Some believe that if we can find a doctrine that meets the standards that have been established by those of authority, we have something that gives us direction for our daily living. Unfortunately, doctrinal affirmations are attempts to put into words what some persons believe is the truth. Such a belief system has not brought greater understanding to life, but has kept many from seeking the inner confirmation of the meaning of life.

We all witness the barriers that separate people from one another. Often the barriers exist within the minds of the individuals themselves. We are taught to think in ways that isolate. We are of a different class, another race, a distant culture, or an unusual religion. The boundaries are rigid. If we attempt to cross them, we find ourselves being strangled to death by the very things designed to preserve our life.

The way of transformation that Jesus exemplified in his life illustrates time and again the infinite worth and dignity of each person. He reached out to others affirming their individuality. He did not prey upon their feeling of failure. He continually sought to purge these feelings of death and slavery forever from the lives of everyone he encountered. It is no accident that Jesus called Judas, who was an Edomite, to be a disciple. Not only was he a disciple, but Judas was to have charge of the money that the group used for their living expenses. He placed trust and faith in one whom Galileans felt was despicable, and untrustworthy.

Judas joined the eleven Galileans, chosen by Jesus to be his inner circle. Judas needed to experience acceptance, affirmation, and a sense of importance.

Jesus taught the simple truth that people are free to choose. Each person has the capacity to make his own choices. Such choices do not have to be approved by anyone, nor must permission be asked in order to choose. Whether they are a husband or a wife, a mother or a father, a son or a daughter, an adult or a child, the choice is always one's own. It is an indelible mark of our humanity. When it is grasped and exercised, we discover the meaning of transformation. Before, we did not know we had a choice, and now, we understand that the choice is always ours.

A fact of life is that the only way we can apprehend the qualities of an identity outside ourselves is by our willingness to lose our own boundaries-outposts of our rugged individualism—and to move out with our imaginations into the experience of that which we desire to perceive.

Loving is boundary-losing. It is the only attitude that will increase an individual's knowledge of reality. In fact, truth does not rest in itself and for itself, but it is something that takes place between two people. Truth happens only in community. The fact is that truth is not an established fact which is unchanging but a continuous unfolding of Creation. Truth is not an abstraction. Truth is the expansion of experience.

We often think that what we believe is the only truth. It is difficult to admit that my truth is truth for me but my neighbor views the world from a different perspective than I. The spot from where we view life is important. It is also important for the other person.

In 1991, two weeks before Christmas, I found myself again confronted by my heart disease. The doctor called to let me know how the last Doppler echogram had turned out. In a very somber voice, he said "Mr. Hipkins," (there was a fifteen to twenty second pause). "I have bad news. You need open heart surgery. Your aortic valve must be replaced. I can suggest a surgeon to contact." I told him I would get back to him tomorrow. I hung up the phone—numb. I couldn't believe what he had just told me. A friend and my wife who had been talking in the living room were suddenly silent. I relayed to them the doctor's message.

Plans were quickly under way. Telephone calls were made to family and friends. Next a surgeon was chosen and an appointment was made to see him at our cardiologist's office in Knoxville. The surgeon examined me and told me that my aortic valve was nearly closed. If I did not have surgery, the longest I could look forward to would be a maximum of five years before I died of congestive heart failure. Since I was only sixty-four, he recommend that I have a metal value.

It would have an indefinite life, but I would have to be on a blood thinner the rest of my life.

My wife and children gathered on the day before my surgery. They went with me to the hospital and we had lunch in the cafeteria before I registered. I was greeted warmly by the nurses in the heart surgery area and I was directed to the room that would be my arena for the next series of events. Friends from our Sevierville, TN, First United Methodist Church, came the night before surgery to hold a prayer vigil in the chapel that would continue around the clock until the surgery was completed the next day at noon. The four-hour surgery was longer than anticipated because I was still bleeding after the surgeon had closed the incisions. The next several days were hectic for my family, but I was not aware of anyone or anything during the first 36 hours.

A major event occurred on Sunday morning. I became conscious very early on Sunday morning. My nurse was sitting by my bed. I managed to get my eyes open. I saw my feet under the covers, but my head wouldn't move. I wanted to say something but no sounds came. I tried to move my leg; nothing happened. I felt as if every ounce of strength had been drained from my body. My mind came alive. I remember saying to myself, "You believe in the Creative Power that pervades all of creation. You have always believed you were within this Creative Power and it was in you. Was there ever a time when I needed it as much as now?" Not even thinking or debating, I said a silent prayer, asking God to manifest his Creative Power. Without it, I seemed utterly unable to move. I closed my eyes. Then I discovered the truth in the idea that we must let go in order to gain. It is in holding on that we lose everything. I let go and just lay waiting for some affirmation of the presence of God.

All of a sudden I was in the midst of my favorite place in our Tennessee woods—in the center of a bare spot in the woods at least 35 feet in diameter. Circled by oaks and hickory, I was lying about five feet off the ground, totally unsupported by anything. My arms were out from my sides as if I was trying to reach a tree on each side. In the midst of this experience I said to myself, "Oh how I need to feel the confirmation of your presence in my own life." As I lay there for an unknown time, slowly, I could feel energy and strength flowing into my body. It was as if I was plugged into the source of power. Then, all at once, I became aware that I was in my bed in the hospital. I opened my eyes and saw the nurse doing some morning chores. He acknowledged my awaking and asked if I wanted anything. I said, "I would like breakfast and coffee." In a few minutes, he brought me a tray. I couldn't really raise up very high but I managed to eat the cereal and drink the coffee. I felt weak but alert and conscious of where I was and what was going on around me. I asked what day it was. The nurse replied, "Sunday." I had been out for two days.

This experience of being out of my body confirmed for me that when we lose the awareness of our attachment to things, we feel more deeply our connection to creation. When I had the peaceful transport out of my body to the woods, I was aware that I was in my body but I didn't feel any attachment to it. I have come to understand that to become aware of oneself requires no effort at all. It isn't necessary to seek it. It is not in seeking that we find it; it is in letting go that we discover the real gifts of life.

Central to a spiritual birth is a rediscovery of self-hood. Jesus of Nazareth outlined the necessity of self-hood. His call to his followers was "to love your neighbor as yourself". It begins with self-understanding, appreciation and respect of self, a celebration of human dignity, honesty, trust and integrity. Without such values the Creative Process has no way of enabling life to grow to wholeness.

I have found a new appreciation for each day and each moment. I awake to be amazed at the opportunity to share in another day with Charlotte and have our moments of intimacy and romance; to speak with my grandchildren and savor the enthusiasm of their exciting lives. I look forward to each opportunity to have a conversation with my son and my daughter. Simply to have the family present for a meal becomes another doxology for another, beautiful, golden day. I will never again take for granted any of the relationships with my family and friends. I look forward to each opportunity to experience that which would never have been, had I not had the wonderful rebirth at the hospital in 1992.

13

Connections

SEE THYSELF

In Thee,
In me,
In all men
There dwelleth the One God:
In all
He suffers,
And he suffers
For all:
In all, everywhere,
See thyself:
Abandon this thy ignorant conceit,
Which holds that thou art separate
from other men.[1]

I believe that the Creative Power at the center of life allows nothing to be excluded. Creation is sustained, animated and connected with/to the Creative Power of life.

If a person who attempts to disconnect herself from others and nature, she will find that life eludes her. However, separation can never be accomplished. Many times, we want to separate ourselves. We delude ourselves in thinking we are disconnected. We are intimately and eternally bound to all. We have been placed on the Circle at our birth. Nothing can remove us from the place where we were birthed.

1. Translated by M.K. Gandhi from Sanskrit poem.

In the United States, we affirm our individual independence of everyone and everything. However, the concept of a single, isolated individual is untenable and impossible. A person cannot isolate himself nor stand as a single person without any relationship to other people.

Many of my actions in life are motivated by the desire to disconnect from others. In fact, I often assert how much I am a separate being capable of making decisions by and for myself. I laud my independence as a person and as a part of creation; yet, there is no way I can disconnect from others. My decisions are never only my own; my decisions always influence and affect everyone on the Circle. What I do or do not choose affects the rain forests, the plight of the Kurds, the devastation in East Timor and my neighbors down the hill. Although, I constantly affirm my independence and individuality, my uniqueness is in relationship to the whole. I am not just unique and separate from others, but I am unique because of my relationship to others. I have a perspective that is essential for an understanding of the Circle and the wisdom that is found on it and within it.

We live in a world that is inner-directed. There seems to be at the basis of all living things-of the universe itself—an inner power (inner force) that pushes forward to birth an ever-expanding universe-a pattern of a living organism and an organizing system. In one sense, you can say that life is self-organizing. The inner force, inner power is a thrust into life that is always present.

From my lifetime of organizing groups and organizations, I believe it is fair to say that organizations are living systems. Of course, it is the people who are the living systems within the organization. Because persons have intelligence, people are capable of choice and change. Machines have no such capacity to change; they run according to the program or design that was developed at their creation by some engineer. At the same time, we have discovered that we live in a universe that is alive, creating and experimenting every second. It is constantly discovering what is possible within the ever-expanding universe. People who live within the universe like order, not continual change and shifting. Yet, people are capable of creative adaptation to changing circumstances. Most of all, they see meaning in life.

One of the natural tendencies in life is to organize—to seek greater levels of complexity and diversity. Humankind is rediscovering its inner connectedness. There are no isolated individuals in our world—though people often feel isolated. There appears to be at the heart of life an inner power that drives a person to seek life. As he seeks more relationships in life, it makes more possibilities available and it increases the diversity of creation.

Many relationships breakup because of arguments about who is right. Yet, when you look around, you see life illustrating that people are busy tinkering, experimenting, playing, as if to say, if it works fine, and if it doesn't work, let's find a way that does work. As we look at the problems confronting us, we discover life's creative power creates more possibilities as it engages with new approaches or ways of organizing. It appears to me that every time we try to make something work, we are creating more possibilities within life. We actually open different windows of opportunity for the future.

Many sociologists tell us that we live in a culture shattered by a lack of consensus. Our praise of individualism has brought us to the brink of cultural suicide. We have shed ourselves of the only force that can integrate a culture—spiritual life. Culture is integrated by religion. When religion grows weak or non-existent there is nothing to integrate the culture. We stand at the crossroads where we must make decisions that will affect untold generations.

The air, the water, the animals, humankind, and the plants, all are dependent upon one another for sustenance and survival. People find their identity and their self-understanding in a tribe—the group into which they are born and among whom they find themselves on the Circle. Their name identifies them and records them in the annals of life. They are separate, yet intimately related and tied to others. They are unique but their uniqueness is derived from their relatedness.

An isolated person has no meaning. From the birthing of life to the transition through the death of the body, we discover meaning and purpose in our relationship with life—life is existence. Existence is all of creation.

There is wholeness in life—a wholeness that filled Jesus' teaching with meaning and significance. He encountered people who had divided life into compartments. They were Israelites, Galileans, Greeks, Romans, Pharisees, Sadducces, Stoics, Essenes, Epicureans and others. They emphasized their own language and their separate cultures. Many nations have evolved myths that illustrate their uniqueness in Creation. They see themselves as the favorite of the Creator. Not realizing that everyone is a special person of the Creator, they base their conclusions on incorrect assumptions. No one person or group occupies a special status in Existence. Israel interprets their election by God to be one of privilege, when in actuality it is one of responsibility. They are given the responsibility to model the intimate connection of Creation to the Creator. Every ritual act and cultural custom sought to affirm that Israel was God's chosen people. Their Holy Book underscores and reiterates this fact in a multitude of stories and events. It is appropriate that Jesus, who became the Christ, would emerge from such a group.

Every act he performed and every teaching expressed his disconnection from his cultural past. When culture becomes hardened and the traditions are conceived to exist for their own purpose, it is time to break with the conventional wisdom of a people. Jesus experienced the separation that occurred among his people. They thought of others as 'those people.' 'Those people' became a designation for persons who were considered different. Jesus attempted to help people understand there were only **people**. Separating themselves from others meant renunciation of the unity of God's creation and emphasizing the virtue of divisiveness. God created the world. Humankind realized on Pentecost, differences are not highlighted in God's understanding of life. Instead, God struck into the midst of the multitude in the most powerful way to enable people to understand one another.

I have become aware that the Creative Power bursts forth when I embrace all creation. When I withdraw and embrace only my own kind, I feel as if I am retreating into an existence of virtual paralysis. Jesus sought to help people understand that when the Edomites were embraced, fellowship was richer and the circle of life was affirmed. The Samaraitans, who were brought into fellowship, found new doors and windows to meaning. When separation is overcome and the unity of creation is understood, the conventional wisdom of a people begins to change. Isolation and separation dissolves. Experiencing a sense of relatedness or oneness with people who are different, I experience the deepest meaning of God's creation-affirmed in the wholeness of life.

One of the most important truths I have experienced is that my view is only a partial perception of truth. This is the most difficult to accept. Truth is not something that rests on itself and for itself. It is something that takes place between persons. Truth happens in community. Truth is not an established fact which is unchanging, but truth is a continuous unfolding of creation; truth is the expanding of experience and meaning.

The expansion of truth is clearly pointed out in the visions of Black Elk. He believed that there are four powers that are essential to life. He taught that if you perceive only one power, it is just a part, a partial truth. A whole person perceives all four. Partialness will destroy. Partialness is the seedbed of bigotry and ideology. It leads to a fragmentation of life and splits families and creates chaos among nations.

Witness today in the USA, the many groups who see the truth only from their particular view. Since it is partial, they act only on partial truth. Yet, they are convinced that they perceive the whole truth. They assert that their view is the correct view. This is the problem of partiality. It always leads to wrong conclusions.

Black Elk instructs us that there are two roads we can travel in life. One is the *red road* that leads to life. The second road is the *black road* that leads to death.

Every group (tribe) has insight and light to share on the journey. For example, the Chinese believe that an understanding of *Feng Shui* is crucial to life. It is a view of wind and water that reveal how life can nurture or cripple contentment, personal growth, health and relationships. An understanding of *Feng Shui* can reverse the negative conditions around us, and make it possible for us to improve our quality of life—and to become happier than ever before in our connections with other people.

Feng Shui explores how connections (*Tao*), balance (*yin* and *yang*), and vitality (*chi*) impact life-and the senses of sight, sound, smell and touch influence behavior. *Feng Shui* is not just about place, but how a person experiences life. To make beneficial changes in our environment, we must first assess our individual needs and experiences. This is another example of how we can learn from other cultures. We discover that there are other ways of thinking that can open the doors to a richer and fuller life. It means that we must move away from the partial views and narrow ways of thinking.

The understanding we have about work also influences our life. When we mention work, what meanings does it evoke for you? If we define it loosely, work is effort expended in order to accomplish something. When people lived as hunters and gatherers, it took three or four days' labor to supply life's necessities. The rest of the time was reserved for social interaction and other satisfying experiences. For most of us today, three or four hours of daily leisure would be considered a treat.

Today "play" is described as "work". We "work out" to tone our bodies; we complete "homework" when taking courses to improve our minds, we work on committees, we work at church and tell our family that dinner is in the works. With our European backgrounds we have grown to expect life to be an exercise of exertion.

Despite the tremendous social changes that have occurred over the centuries, the foundation of human needs has not changed. What is changed are the prerequisites. If we could stand back and see the road stretching before us as we end the twentieth century, we could acknowledge how we have separated life into two paths: the path of "things", the Black Road, and the path of "feelings", the Red Road. The Red Road celebrates experiences and values of positive emotional connections. On the "things" path, material realities supersede emotional ones. We cut ourselves off from emotional responses. The Black Road objectifies goals and holds in highest regard pursuits that have measurable results. Very often the focus on "things" have the following four results:

1. Isolation—People develop a feeling of being disconnected from others and this is caused by a focus devoid of human relationships.

2. Tension—it can cause us to act inappropriately with and toward others. It can trigger depression. For example, fluorescent lighting can cause tension. This is because we are designed biologically to be outside in sunlight, which differs from most indoor lighting because it contains all colors of the visible spectrum. Sunlight spurs the production of a hormone that produces an euphoric or optimistic state. A lack of exposure to sunlight can lead to a type of depression called Seasonal Affective Disorder (SAD). By not experiencing natural light, we are denying ourselves a natural opiate that can cause us to be empathetic and careful in our communications—not tense, abrupt and charged.

3. Strain—it separates us from being in touch with ourselves and to interactions with others.

4. Obsession—it witnesses that our life is controlled by the obligations of work or family—a feeling that is fueled by clutter. Papers scattered everywhere can create a sense of fear for the individual of not being able to complete obligations. Such anxiety is detrimental to both physical and mental health and ultimately compromises the ability to interact with other people.

To permit life to flow as naturally as the unfolding of a flower, we must heed the message programmed into our biological nature. By addressing our needs, we lessen life's pressures, allowing us to have interactions with others and ourselves. Life can be improved when we remedy the assaults on our contentment.

If Black Elk, the Chinese philosophers, and Jesus of Nazareth can enable us to see a new vision of life connected to all of Creation, we will have tapped the universe's deepest source of wisdom for humankind.

14

Don't Set Limits on What God Can Do

"The reason for living now is not because time is short, but because now is where life is."[1]

I have faced situations in my life that seemed impossible to solve. One of the situations I confronted in my very first two weeks at college threatened to destroy me. I almost let it.

After a number of tests the first week at college, we went to have a session with our academic advisor. This person was assigned to monitor our curriculum during our period at Ohio Wesleyan. After the battery of tests, I decided that a career in the foreign service was the most appealing. As we mapped out my study program, French would be one of the very important subjects to master since it was the language of diplomacy throughout the world; therefore, I registered for French 101. I had studied only two years of Latin. My high school offered no other foreign language course.

Little did I realize what was in store for me in the next several weeks. The first two class sessions of French were interesting. I was looking forward to learning a new language. I was spending more time on this course than any other. The second week of class, we had a test. The next class session as I picked up my test, the professor said as he handed it to me, "Hipkins, you will be lucky to pass this course. I was stunned by the "F" on the test. The next several classes he seemed to focus on me for answers to his questions in French. Often he embarrassed me before the whole class. I was determined that he would not drive me out of my chosen career. I studied like a demon the rest of the term. The result was a D—in French.

---

1. Pelgrim, Mark, *And A Time To Die, p.124-125.*

When I got my grade, I decided it was time to reevaluate my career goals. Something else would seem more appropriate. Eventually, I choose to prepare for the ministry. However, as I contemplated theological school, I was very afraid of failing Greek or Hebrew. I had to find a school that would not require them for graduation. Boston University, School of Theology was such a school.

After I graduated and was appointed to a local church, I found myself on a different career path. The new path led to foreign missionary service. In the midle of our missionary orientation, we had a week of linguistic training. At this point the decision had not been made where we would serve in Asia. As the linguistic training developed, twelve us were separated from the group because we did not seem to have the aptitude of the rest of the candidates. We were the slow-learning class and received special attention. I did have a hearing problem because in the Army, I lost my ability to hear the soprano and tenor tones. This was the result of being part of a 57mm gun crew. Half way through the linguistic training, a letter arrived informing us that we would be going to Yale University, Institute of Far Eastern Languages to learn Chinese. I was amazed. Earlier, a language aptitude examination had been administered to each of us. I was in the 12th percentile. This suggested that I was among a group of persons who had limited ability to learn a language. I went to the director of the linguistic training to talk over these recent revelations. I raised the question of the wisdom of someone with my aptitude being sent to learn Chinese. It seemed to me that it is almost a waste of money. This is a very difficult language for an English-speaker to learn. He shared with me his insights. He said that motivation cannot be overlooked. After all, I had the motivation to learn. If I really applied myself, he believed that I could get through the course. We talked for an hour or so, discussing the fact that with God's presence and the power of commitment, we should not set limits on our accomplishments.

In January, 1964, we found ourselves in New Haven facing the challenge of learning spoken Chinese. Charlotte, fortunately, has a gift for learning languages. She was an honor student at Ohio Wesleyan in German. She is a first generation American who spoke only German at home until she went to elementary school. This enabled her to excel. I was a different story.

Who should be one of our teachers but someone just like my former French professor. Since I had difficulty hearing and would often miss what the teacher said in class, Edward, one the Chinese instructors, would seek to embarrass me on many occasions. In spite of his attitude and my own limitations, I earned a certificate from the Far Eastern Institute at Yale University. It hangs on my wall as a reminder that regardless of the gifts we have been given, nothing can replace the commitment to succeed. We can do what we purpose to do. There is no defeat for those who refuse to be defeated. Others might try to destroy our self-image, or try to rob us of our dreams but these cannot be destroyed without our consent. I almost allowed the French professor to determine my life. Faith, hope and commitment can turn an impossible situation into a moment of victory.

There are two other handicaps that have been with me since WW II. Because of the serious case of histoplasmosis[2] that I acquired, I have had a diminished capacity in one lung. I have learned to pace my walking and stair-climbing to allow my lungs to work normally. I have limited my swimming and other physical activities that require adequate lung capacity. One learns he has these limitations. that will not change and you must learn to live with them. The other problem that I have lived with in my adult life is a weakness in my feet and legs. I was hurt during WW II, and the discomfort and pain that I have in my lower legs is a result of this injury. Sometime my legs hurt so badly that I have no alternative but to sit down. I am unable to walk more than 20 minutes if we go shopping in a mall or grocery store. I excuse myself and sit in the mall or go out to the car. In 1947, the VA made special braces for my feet. Each one weighed about two pounds. They were made out of steel. For a number of years I wore them regularly and they really helped. The difficulty was that they cut my shoes in half. What were the alternatives? There were none. Through the years, I have had a continuing battle with both of these disabilities. Life seems to give the strength to deal with what life passes out to us. I am grateful for the opportunities I have had, in spite of my own physical limitations.

2. This is a fungus disease that grows in the lungs. It deposits calcium as a residue where it has grown. It can be fatal.

15

Which Values Do I Choose?

I discovered on my journey that I had to decide what values I wanted to pursue. Each value is not of equal importance. The temptation is to choose one that has immediate satisfaction but long term consequences. I believe that I was fortunate to be confronted with a major choice of values when I returned from India in 1961. Actually, the conflict in my mind and soul began long before I went to Asia. I sensed a conflict in my goals and values as the new congregation began to grow in Montgomery, Ohio. I was tempted by the lure of larger churches and more salary. I could close my eyes and imagine the acclamation and praise that came with such success. Real or imagined, it made very little difference. One's response would make all the difference in the world. My trip to Asia was an attempt to clarify the values I ought to place at the center of my life. Obviously, I had committed myself to the pastoral ministry, but it seemed to me that my commitment was partial. I was tempted by the acclaim, the success and the financial rewards that follow achievements. I found myself much more deeply in the mainstream of American culture than I had intended.

Because of my trip to Asia in 1961 and the soul searching that followed, I found myself confronted with a choice of values. I understood that the choice I made on the day Henry Hitt Crane brought me face to face with Jesus Christ that my whole life was involved with that commitment. The question was whether I could have financial and personal acclaim and keep my faith whole? In other words, could I have my cake and eat it to. I must now make a choice that would determine my future. Would I choose success in worldly terms or in faith terms? Could I commit myself wholly to Jesus Christ?

You will recall the confrontation I had when a young girl asked me if I had ever sold everything to follow Christ. I may have turned red with embarrassment. I cannot remember my answer. I think I tried to explain away some of the impact of what I had said to the group. Her question would haunt me in the months to come until we finally sold everything we had in 1963, to follow the leading of the Spirit of Light that had become so bright in our life.

During this period, 1962–63, Charlotte and I returned to some of our roots. She was helping recruit young people for missionary service through the Women's Society in our District and in our Conference. We were both constantly confronted with this basic decision of the values we put at the center of our life.

I returned more and more to Jesus and his guidance in my search. During this period of searching, I found myself returning to familiar stories in the Bible for guidance. One Biblical story stands out clearly in my mind from those days of torment and struggle.

It is found in Luke 4:1-14 in the New Testament.

The sun was unrelenting. The temperature was rising. It was as if one's head was in an oven. The air was so heavy, it was hard to breathe. The perspiration had grown less and less each day. His throat was parched. His eyes itched from their dryness. He crouched all afternoon in the shadow of a huge stone in the midst of nothing but sand. As he looked through his half-open eyes, he tried to discern some movement of life in the distance. All he could see was sand and barren land in every direction. The first few weeks he found tolerable. As the fourth week approached, he found it more difficult to pray. He could not keep his mind focused on God or love. Each time he swallowed, his parched throat ached for a drink. In the midst of this, something happened! Suddenly, he felt the presence of denial, of self, hate and negativism. How could he? How? His thirst threatened to overcome his body and mind. Thus he felt the presence of denial. He heard in his mind "If only you will bow down and worship me, all this will be yours. If only you would deny God, he does not give you drink. At the end of his temptation in the wilderness, Jesus answered the Spirit of Evil that confronted him. He said, "It is also written that I must not prove the Eternal, My God." J. Middleton Murray commented that here the word of the Creator was spoken. "The Spirit of Evil, who is the Spirit that forever denies, left him and never returned."[1] When one focuses on the negative view, the spirit of denial, the opportunity for a new birth of consciousness is impossible.

Carl Jung said that imitating Christ is not the same thing as "aping" Christ. Rather, it is imitating what Christ always did: **he was true to his authentic nature**. The divine consciousness imbued Jesus with a strong ego, a hollow reed

1. Murray, J. Middleton, *Jesus-Man of Genius*, p.34.

that was the channel for the light of the world. That light was the basis of Jesus' actions.

Jesus emerged from the Desert focused on a new message. He had discovered that to get along with other people, **he must find the rhythm that harmonizes with them and then bring these separate rhythms into harmony.** He had to find within himself that which filled his inner void and addressed it. He did not say anything about being "nice" to an enemy or letting someone walk over you.

Some say that Jesus was primarily a teacher of belief, or more precisely, of what has to be believed in order to be (whole) saved. Others stress that Jesus was teaching a new moral code consisting of high specific demands: love, justice, gold rule, brotherhood of man. Both views contain an element of truth. However, both views are only partial.

I believe that Jesus was not primarily a teacher of either correct beliefs or right morals. He was a teacher of a WAY, a path. He introduced a life of transformation that bears testimony to the Creative Process. He challenged the contemporary culture by calling into question the encultured religion—a religion that had accommodated to the culture and was increasingly shaped by those who were the beneficiaries of the culture. Once religion is captured by culture, it becomes a legitimator of a way of life rather than the innovator of new ways of living. The culture of first century Judaism was seen as the center of identity and purity. Jesus opposed the perception of the Jewish world of his day—a world in which one culture was viewed as the center of existence.

He perceived reality as open and compassionate. Jesus did not come with a new requirement, but an invitation to see things as they are-love, harmony, and balance as the basis of life. He taught an alternative way of being, and an alternative consciousness shaped by Spirit. It was not to be dependent on the dominant consciousness of a particular culture.

Jesus believed that the miracle of birth into the new consciousness that had happened to him would happen to all people; the Spirit would be instantly poured out upon all people as he proclaimed the mystery of the Kingdom of God. I, too, could have such a rebirth.

If I intend to be a disciple of Jesus, it must be clear that I am seeking to follow Jesus' teachings and not what others have proposed he taught. For example, John's message was one of "repentance". But "repentance" is not a word that Jesus used. The significance of Jesus' words has been impoverished because tradition has allowed many words used by others to be attributed to Jesus. Jesus asserted that people need to turn and be changed, as Jesus himself had turned and been changed. As people are reborn, the world is reborn. J. Middleton Murray pointed out in his book that this "was and is and ever will be the wonderful news of Jesus". People have seldom believed in it, though they have believed in things concerning him far more incredible than this. Murray put it in very simple words, "Jesus said that men had only to believe the wonderful news for it to be true; they had only to believe that they were sons of God to be sons of God; they had only to believe that God was their Father. That was all: only to believe."[2] The secret to all that Jesus taught is so simple. "You must be perfect as your Father in Heaven is perfect." People are to become one with God; just as God makes His sun rise on the evil and the good, so the Son of God loves the evil and the good alike. This is the center of Jesus profoundest teaching: it is no less than people must be God-they are one with God. People are one with God not tomorrow or after they die but in this moment of their existence.

It was at this point that I realized Jesus emphasized "**you are**" rather than "you ought", or "you will be". He taught people that **you are** light, hope, love, forgiveness, brothers, sons of God, the promise, and more. The spirit that never denies asserts a positive and hopeful vision for life. I must become conscious of who I am and understand that God expects me to be myself. My integrity demands my faithfulness to my "ground of being", to my calling to be my authentic self.

Jesus deliberately chose the way of suffering and death; it was forced on him by the consciousness of his own personal self-worth and personal mission. Through the centuries it has been understood in a way that has confused many persons. To many people, Jesus' self-sacrifice is understood to be of little consequence. Formulations change, but the spiritual reality is the same. Isn't it true, we have a hard time to believe that a man is capable of such a supreme and imaginative act? The Christian affirmation is a clear statement of the act of a man, Jesus. This sacrifice was the manifestation of God and of Man in all its fullness.

Because of the influence of the Society of Friends on my life, and my Native American heritage, I find that I have come to appreciate Jesus through a different set of eyes. When I began my journey, it was history and tradition that set the boundaries of belief. As my journey continued through the years, I have been introduced to a mystical approach that caught not only my imagination, but has written itself deeply into my spiritual experience. I believe that we will never understand Jesus only through history or through the Bible. Jesus has come to me in the silent moments of expectant waiting. He has spoken to me in both quiet moments and in the roar of the crowds. It is here that I have received what Light

---

2. Murray, JMOG, p. 39.

I have sought to guide me on this journey. When I have waited for Him, he has come to me and brought the gifts of love and hope.

It is presumptive to suggest what is unique about Jesus. Yet, I must presume that I have encountered what I understand to be His most unique characteristic. All that is unique in Jesus derives directly from his power to love; this came from his knowledge of God as a loving father, his knowledge of himself as God's son, his knowledge that the coming kingdom of God consisted in a unity of humankind, his knowledge that the way to enter the kingdom is to know himself, and to live as a child of God. Jesus acknowledged this is available to every person. This is the birthright of humankind. This is the nature of the Kingdom he proclaimed.

Another characteristic of Jesus' thought which has grown in my experience is that there is purpose in the harmony of life. In the moment in which I became aware of this, I was reborn into the Kingdom and I acquired knowledge of the creative power of God. I am intimately connected to everything in creation. Where there is love, there I am. Where there is pain and suffering, I am there. Where people reach out in compassion, I share in a moment of harmony. Rebirth is the affirmation of a living, unbroken unity between a member of the Kingdom and God himself.

Jesus taught a politics of compassion. In the first century there was social turmoil in the Jewish world. Various groups and classes were in disagreement with each other. There was a widening conflict with Rome. Jesus sought to transform his social world by creating an alternative community, structured on compassion, with norms based on inclusiveness, acceptance, love and peace (*shalom).* He understood that the life of the Spirit was incarnational. This life must be embodied in the daily life of people.

I believe that the dominant values of contemporary American life, affluence, appearance, power, competition, consumption and individualism are different from anything recognizably Christian. Jesus confronts those values with a conflicting set of values. If we are to take Jesus seriously, we have no choice but to be like him.

The world needs people with courage and vision. Such vision must be of a life lived on the boundary of spirit and culture. Entrance into such a life begins with the birth of the spirit in one's life. When Christ calls a person, he bids him to come and die. These words of Bonhoffer echo down the hallways of history. If one is to have a rebirth from the world of conventional wisdom, to a new way of being, surely it begins with a new life.

The core element in the new life that became clear to me is **spirit**. The dominant quality is compassion. It is both a feeling and a way of living. An additional element in the new life is a dialectical relationship to culture. The new life creates a new culture and a new community—an alternative community. It calls the church to lead in this creation of an alternative culture in our time.

Jesus' view is one view of a large number of humanly constructed maps of reality. But, we cannot live according to every map. We must choose one to follow on our journey. I celebrate the fact that my wife and I had the insight and courage to choose the one Jesus presented to us in all the turmoil in our lives. This has made all the difference in our journey.

16

Signs Along the Way

Each person has in his mind something he hopes to achieve. He envisions for himself some life style, achievement, or goal that he hopes to accomplish at some point in his life, even if those goals are not clearly formed. This is part of the human search for meaning and purpose in life. I have shared with you my dreams, my decisions, and the consequent life that evolved as I turned my life over to God.

We are all conditioned to want something. Everyone is included in this wanting of something. Everything in a person's thought system knows, in one form or another, wanting. Wanting is one of the greatest deceptions. Our lives are dominated by wanting. We believe that a meaningful life is something we have to want. Therefore, when we put energy into getting; we do not have energy to put into a relationship with the Creative Process (God).

I have discovered in my life and commend to you this crucial truth. There is a gift that comes to us without wanting. We think it is something we have to achieve or acquire. The fact is it already exists. Why do we want something that is already ours? It is this that I share with you. This is my greatest discovery that occurred on my way to Borneo and back. When I waited in silence for some confirmation, some indication of direction, it was then that God emerged in my life and thought. I waited for something that I did not know. I waited for something that I did not possess, or so I thought. Only to discover, God had already claimed me and was deep within my life. This was the insight and understanding that emerged as I wrestled with Bonhoeffer's challenge to open my life to God and allow Him to direct my journey.

During this sojourn to the jungles of Borneo, there emerged in my life certain guidelines that have enabled me to experience the continuing assurance of the constant guidance of my life by God. I commend to you the following list as essential affirmations for a fulfilled and meaningful life.

1. Humankind has the capacity for self-reflection.

Animals react to life situations. Humankind is a "decider." People are not locked in; therefore they can reflect on their situation and make fresh choices. When persons see their actions in the mirror of self-reflecting knowing, they become self-directing agents of their own evolution. People are not compelled to choose violent values. They willingly choose or reject them. They can choose other values. The choice is up to the individual.

2. A person's life should be rooted in a whole-life view of Creation.

In Western societies, the materialistic-scientific mindset has dominated life. In this view what is real is the material world as perceived by the senses and organized by the intellect. It must be pointed out that a fragmented view of life is not only incorrect, it leads to a whole series of conclusions about life that are wrong. The materialistic-scientific view has led to a fragmentation of life in most dimensions. Today, we have come to understand that empty space is not empty, but is filled with immense amounts of energy. The universe is a unified living system. There is a profound wholeness and interconnection that is the basic fact of existence. People are to be viewed not as separate beings, but as individuals who are intimately involved with one another in the deep web of life.

3. Because of the interconnection of people, all relationships are sacred.

We must bring into balance all the relationships in our world. This perspective will bridge differences, connect people, celebrate diversity, harmonize efforts, and look for high common ground. This perspective is all-inclusive. Every dimension of Creation is included.

4. Non-violence must become the dominant value that pervades relationships in all dimensions.

Humans must renounce violence as an instrument or means of control and power. This is not a conclusion that is lightly taken. It is based on assumptions that are affirmed as the basis of life. These assumptions emerge from the insights that have been discovered at various points on my journey. These insights are:

A. Every action is woven into the ecology of the universe.

Everything we do or do not do matters. We can poison life. This has been happening though our indiscriminate use of pesticides and fungicides. Sustainable agriculture is not an option. Stewardship of creation is essential. Conservation of resources is demanded if the integrity of Creation is to be affirmed.

B. Consciousness is the integrative power in the Creative Process.

We see this in the experience of Jesus of Nazareth. His inner experience enlarged his perception of who he was, and what he is and will be. In a rebirth of consciousness, we experience a confirmation of our self-worth. With it comes a sense of being part of the primary quality of the cosmos. Consciousness is as fundamental as space, time and matter. It is the fundamental component of reality. Once we experience the depth of our relationship to the cosmic consciousness, the individualism that occupied our attention crumbles and we find ourselves immersed in the Creative Process itself.

C. Retribution must be replaced by restoration and growth.

The Creative Process is one of continual rebirth. An essential aspect of it is love. The focus is on growth and not on punishment. Renewal of life is positive not negative.

5. All that exists is integral to the larger body of life.

Cooperation, not competition, is the basis of the relationship of people to one another in the quest for a sustainable life.

6. Each person is responsible for the well-being of the world.

Freedom and fulfillment of life is actualized only in specific ways. At the tribal level humankind must rise to a sustainable harmony with the differences that are given by life. This means that each culture is essential to the whole of humankind. All cultures live in the Lodge of the Spirit.

7. Mutual dependence is a fundamental value that describes our relationship to others and to Creation.

I affirm I am dependent upon other human beings and they are dependent upon me. I must become fully aware of my obligation to each person I meet. I am called to manifest acceptance, affirmation and love.

Borneo was the climax of an exciting search that began many years ago. Friends and understanding individuals we met along the way joined hands with us; they guided us past the pitfalls and impediments along the way.

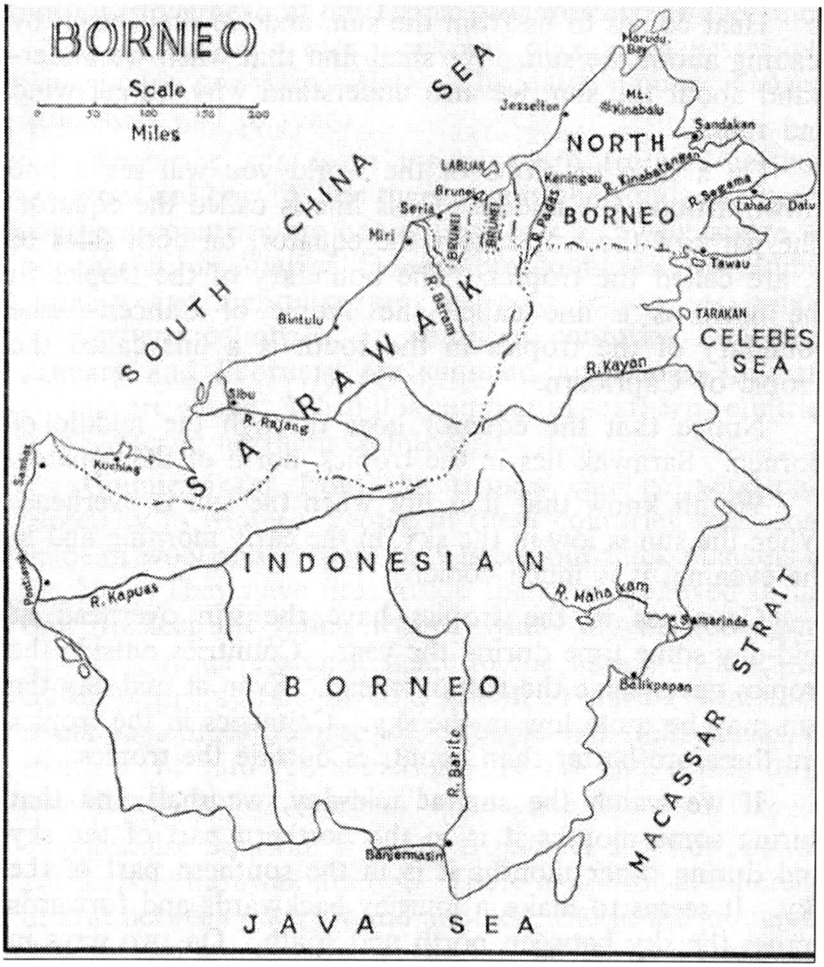
BORNEO
Scale
0
50
100
150
200
Miles
SOUTH CHINA SEA
Marudu Bay
Mt. Kinabalu
Jesselton
Sandakan
NORTH BORNEO
LABUAN
Keningau
R. Kinabatangan
Brunei
R. Segama
Lahad Datu
Seria
BRUNEI
Miri
R. Padas
Tawau
R. Baram
SARAWAK
TARAKAN
Bintulu
CELEBES SEA
R. Kayan
Sibu
R. Rajang
Kuching
INDONESIAN BORNEO
R. Kapuas
R. Mahakam
Samarinda
Balikpapan
MACASSAR STRAIT
R. Barito
Banjermasin
JAVA SEA

0-595-30845-7

Printed in the United Kingdom
by Lightning Source UK Ltd.
121225UK00001B/314

9 780595 308453